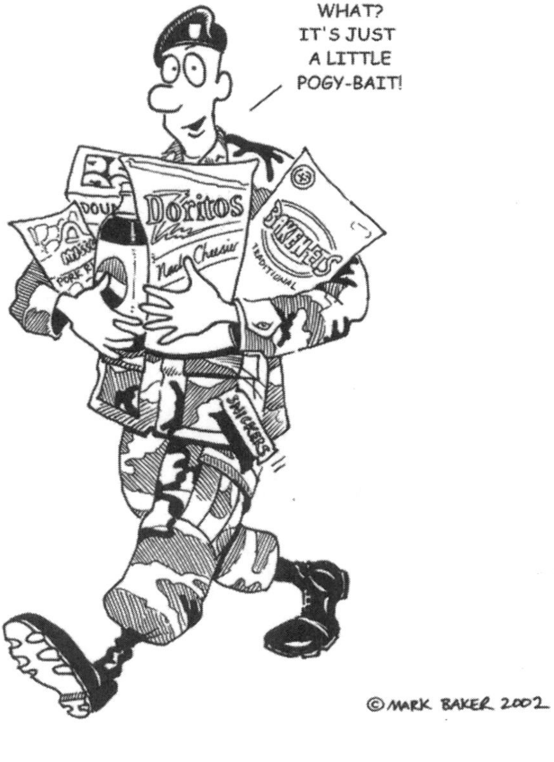
WHAT? IT'S JUST A LITTLE POGY-BAIT!
Doritos
SNICKERS
©MARK BAKER 2002

Forward:

I ran into a group of young men and women in the Mall the other day – I knew they were Soldiers even though they were all in civvies. (It wasn't the hair-cuts, there's just something special about Soldiers, you know?) Anyway, I asked them if they were familiar with the cartoon, "Pvt. Murphy." Their reply was, "Of course, *we're in the Army!*" As if to say that everyone in the Army reads Pvt. Murphy! I wish that was indeed the case, but I know better. Nevertheless, those Soldiers made my day.

I've been drawing Pvt. Murphy cartoons for over 10 years now. At the time of this book's printing the cartoon is in its fourth year as a weekly feature in the Army Times Newpaper. For those who are interested in such things (some are) I'm glad to report that while the amount of negative feedback I receive has remained about the same, the amount of positive feedback I'm getting has greatly increased. I don't know if this is because I took to heart some of the more "constructive" negative letters and e-mails that came my way or if people realize that I really don't mean any harm. (And that I'm not going away.)

I think MAJ Dave Daigle, the Editor-in-Chief of ARMOR magazine put it best when he wrote in the Jan-Feb 2002 issue of ARMOR Magazine, "An institution, organization, or person that cannot tolerate humor, or lacks a sense of humor, is often revealed as insecure or unsure." The Army is far too fine an institution to be insecure or unsure, so lighten up already! You know who you are!

For those of you who like the cartoon: Murphy and I thank you! You ROCK! It is because of you all that this 3rd book is possible!

For those of you who hate me and my silly cartoon: Why did you buy this book? If it was a gift - give it back to whoever gave it to you, they probably *like* Pvt. Murphy!

But seriously, I cannot express in words the amount of admiration I have for all service members, especially those who are serving overseas. I hope that my cartoons bring you a laugh or at least a smile from time to time.

God bless you all,

Mark Baker
12 Feb 2005

Also available:

Book I: "Pvt. Murphy's Law"

Pvt. Murphy's Law
By Mark Baker

Book II: "PV-2 Murphy"

PV-2 MURPHY
THE ADVENTURE CONTINUES
A "PVT MURPHY'S LAW"
COLLECTION BY MARK BAKER

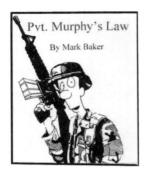

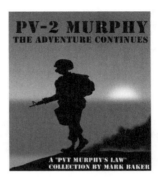

For order information contact Flat Earth Comix
FlatEarthComix@aol.com

Come visit Murphy online at http://www.pvtmurphy.com

1st printed March 2005
ISBN: 0-9679357-2-5

United Book Press
1807 Whitehead Rd
Baltimore, MD 21207

Distributed by Byrrd Enterprises, INC.
1302 Layfayette Drive
Alexandria, VA 22308
1-800-628-0901 (703) 765-5626 fax (703)768-4086

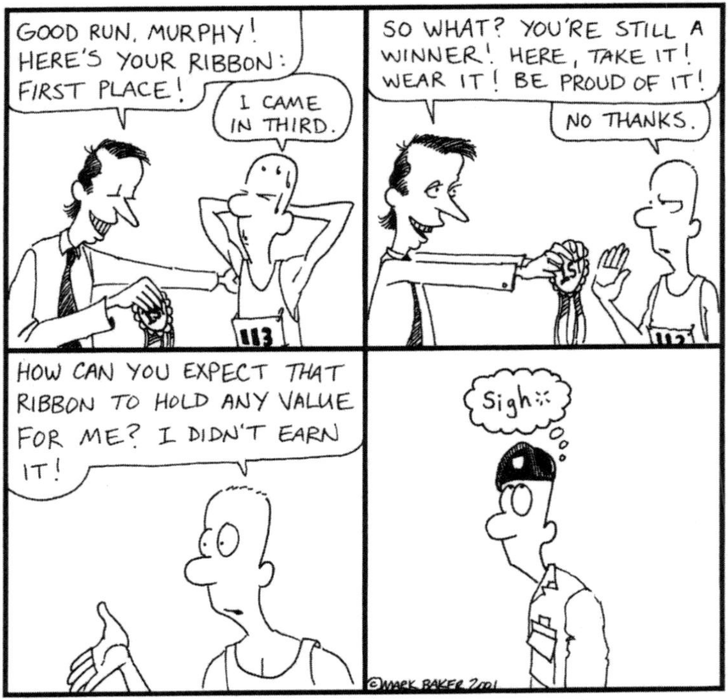
GOOD RUN, MURPHY! HERE'S YOUR RIBBON: FIRST PLACE!
I CAME IN THIRD.
SO WHAT? YOU'RE STILL A WINNER! HERE, TAKE IT! WEAR IT! BE PROUD OF IT!
NO THANKS.
HOW CAN YOU EXPECT THAT RIBBON TO HOLD ANY VALUE FOR ME? I DIDN'T EARN IT!
Sigh
©MARK BAKER 2001

MAJ Tom W. Collins writes:

You think you're funny, but you're not. All you're doing is fermenting stereotypes and widening the gulf between officers and NCO's. Thanks for serving your country.

SFC Baker, I'm sure you know that the military has a regulation about service members speaking out against official DoD or Service policies. This week's cartoon commentary on the beret seems to violate that regulation. You should know better, but I'm going to see what the lawyers tell me. I should be back in contact with you soon.

PFC MURPHY

Code among PFCs

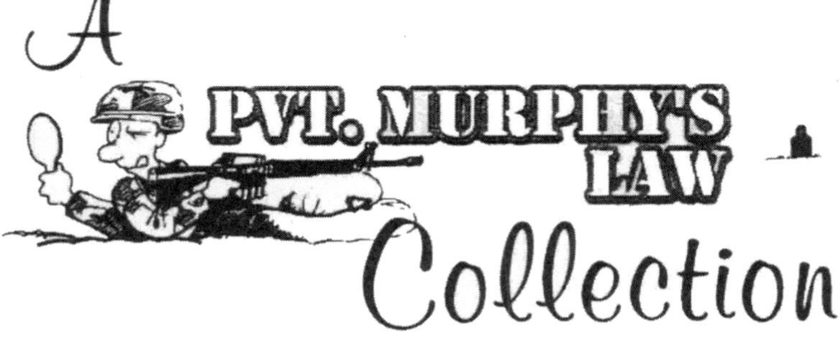
A
PVT. MURPHY'S
LAW
Collection

By Mark Baker

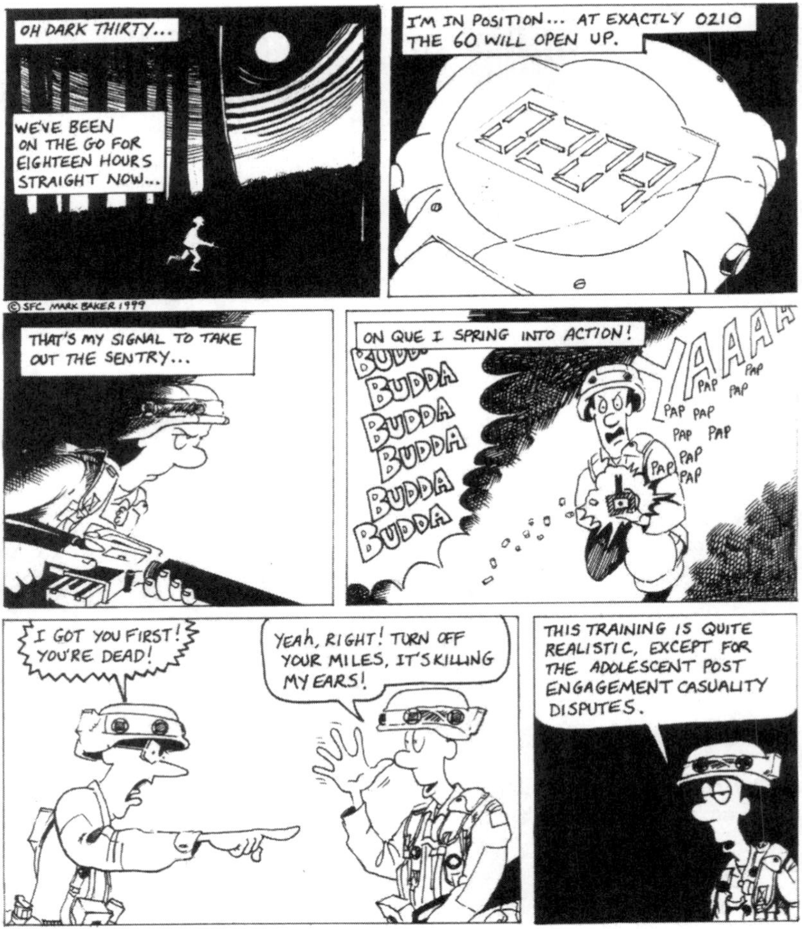
OH DARK THIRTY...
WE'VE BEEN ON THE GO FOR EIGHTEEN HOURS STRAIGHT NOW...
I'M IN POSITION... AT EXACTLY 0210 THE 60 WILL OPEN UP.
0209
© SFC. MARK BAKER 1999
THAT'S MY SIGNAL TO TAKE OUT THE SENTRY...
ON QUE I SPRING INTO ACTION!
BUDDA BUDDA BUDDA BUDDA BUDDA BUDDA
YAAAAH
PAP PAP PAP PAP PAP PAP PAP PAP PAP PAP PAP
I GOT YOU FIRST! YOU'RE DEAD!
Yeah, RIGHT! TURN OFF YOUR MILES, IT'S KILLING MY EARS!
THIS TRAINING IS QUITE REALISTIC, EXCEPT FOR THE ADOLESCENT POST ENGAGEMENT CASUALITY DISPUTES.

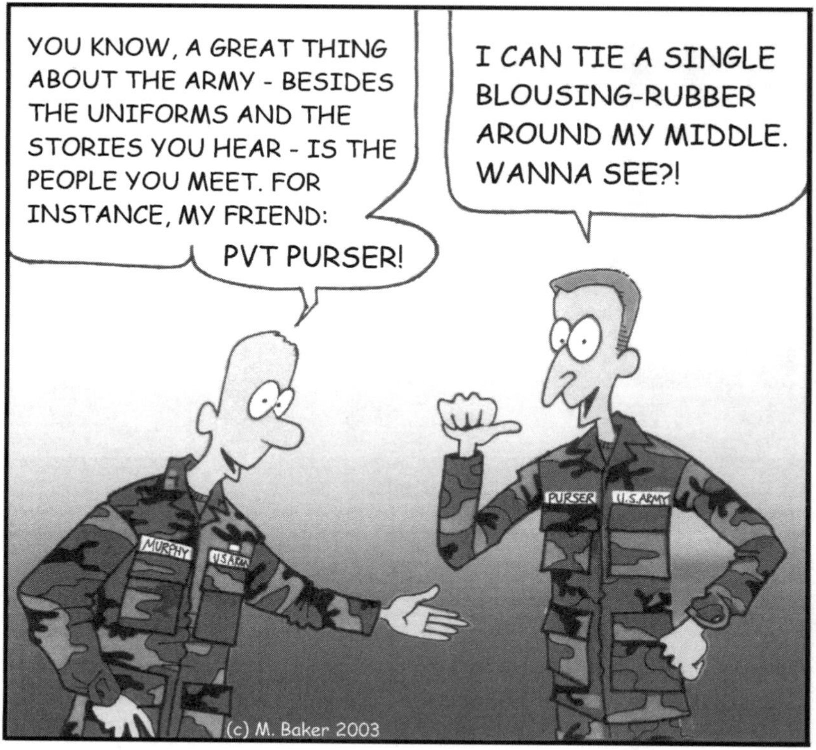
YOU KNOW, A GREAT THING ABOUT THE ARMY - BESIDES THE UNIFORMS AND THE STORIES YOU HEAR - IS THE PEOPLE YOU MEET. FOR INSTANCE, MY FRIEND:
PVT PURSER!
I CAN TIE A SINGLE BLOUSING-RUBBER AROUND MY MIDDLE. WANNA SEE?!
MURPHY
PURSER
U.S.ARMY
(c) M. Baker 2003

Chris Purser is a Blackhawk pilot now, last I heard he can still do that blousing rubber trick.

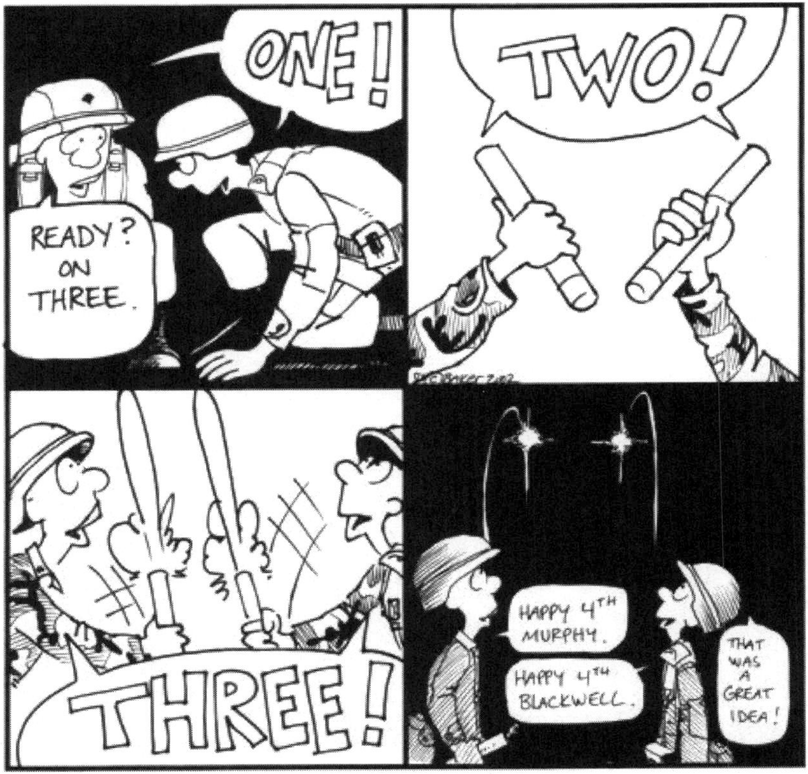
ONE!
READY? ON THREE.
TWO!
THREE!
HAPPY 4TH MURPHY.
HAPPY 4TH BLACKWELL.
THAT WAS A GREAT IDEA!

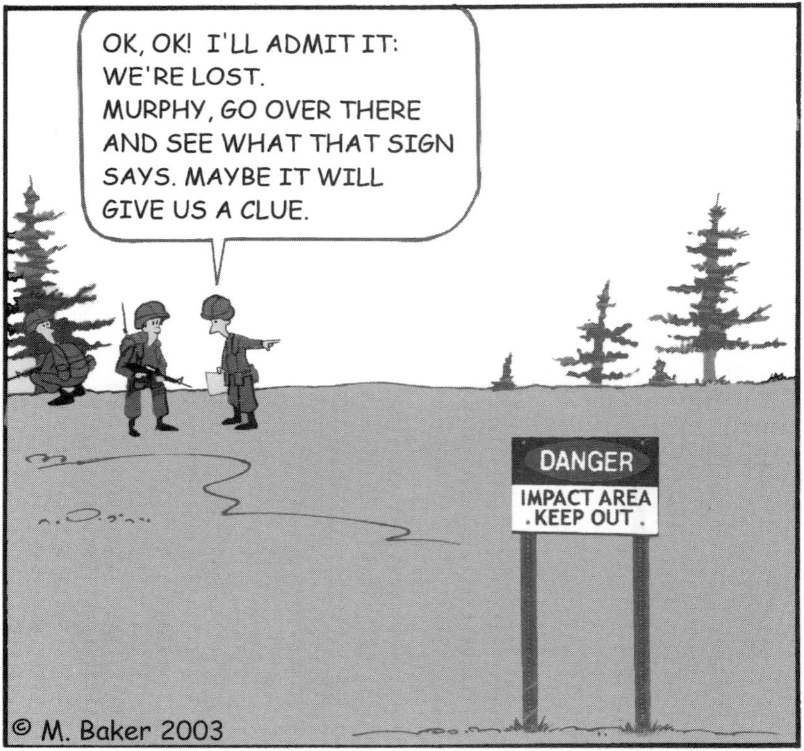
OK, OK! I'LL ADMIT IT:
WE'RE LOST.
MURPHY, GO OVER THERE
AND SEE WHAT THAT SIGN
SAYS. MAYBE IT WILL
GIVE US A CLUE.
DANGER
IMPACT AREA
. KEEP OUT .
© M. Baker 2003

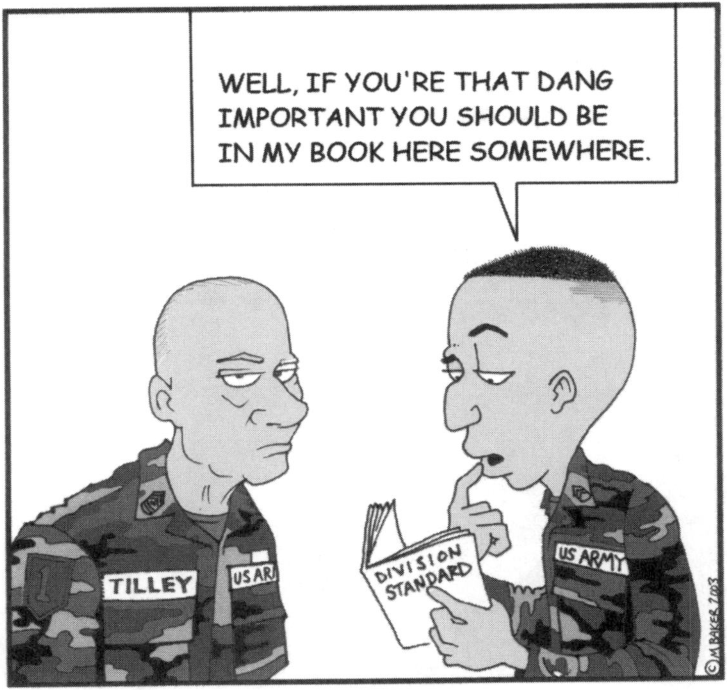
WELL, IF YOU'RE THAT DANG IMPORTANT YOU SHOULD BE IN MY BOOK HERE SOMEWHERE.
TILLEY
US AR
US ARMY
DIVISION STANDARD
©M BAKER 2003

Every now and then I get handed a cartoon idea. If you have ever had the privilege of seeing SMA Tilley in person, you might be familiar with the story he tells about running into a SSG - "With the biggest head you've ever seen" - who didn't know he was talking to the Sergeant Major of the Army. Shortly after this one was published I was contacted by an NCO on the SMA's staff. SMA Tilley liked the cartoon so much he wanted a copy. I sent the original.

I received an e-mail about the following cartoon asking if I was putting down female Officers. That was not the case at all. I drew this particular cartoon for a lady that I hold in very high regard. COL Browning was the Chief of Staff at Ft. Huachuca, AZ. I drew this cartoon for her as a retirement gift. (Her staff helped out with some photos of her office and I added in the MORSE key because of her enlisted background.)

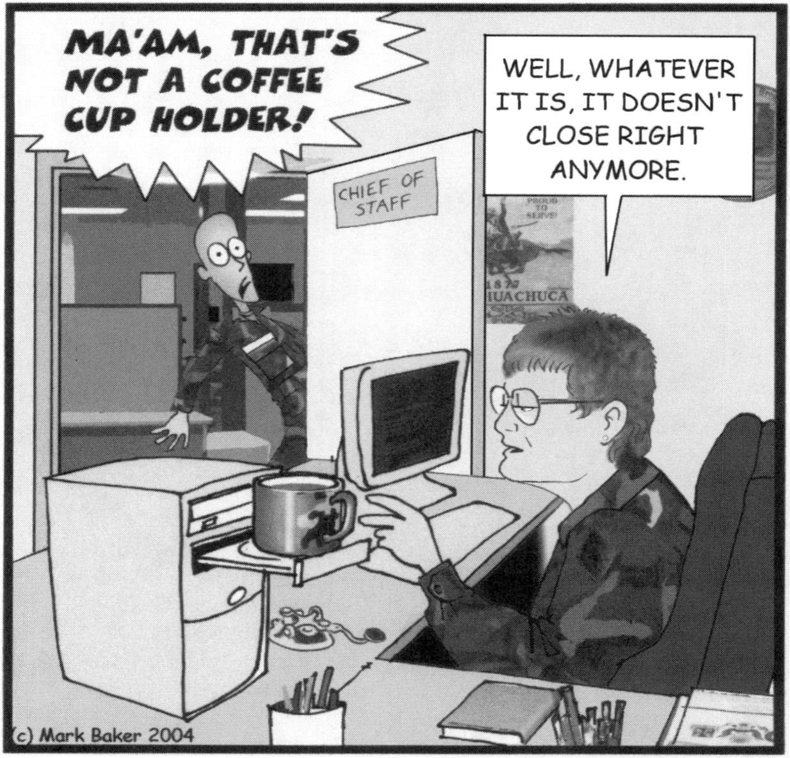
MA'AM, THAT'S NOT A COFFEE CUP HOLDER!
WELL, WHATEVER IT IS, IT DOESN'T CLOSE RIGHT ANYMORE.
CHIEF OF STAFF
HUACHUCA
(c) Mark Baker 2004

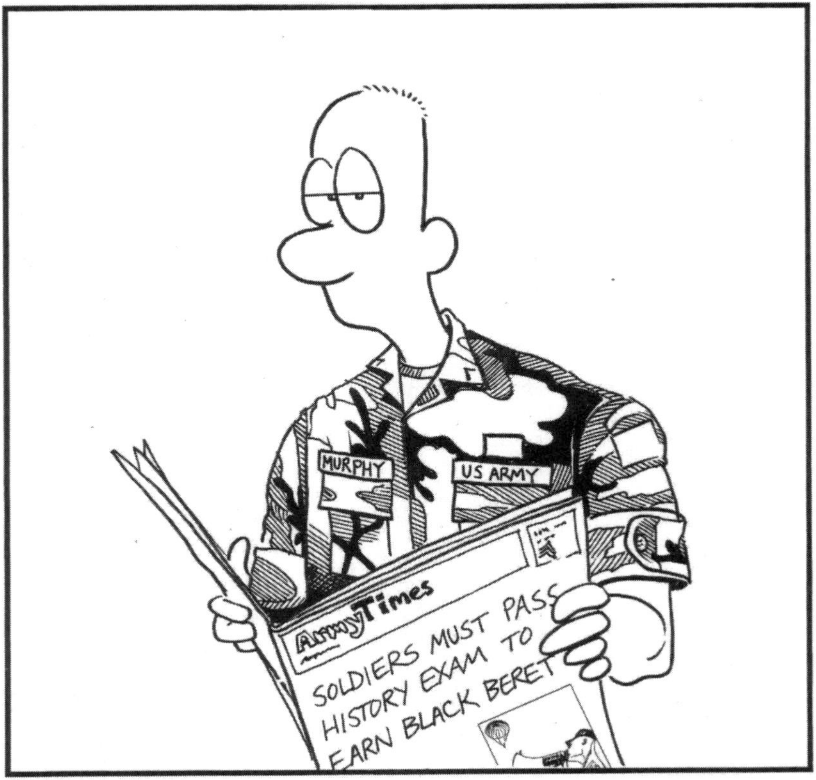
MURPHY
US ARMY
Army Times
SOLDIERS MUST PASS
HISTORY EXAM TO
EARN BLACK BERET

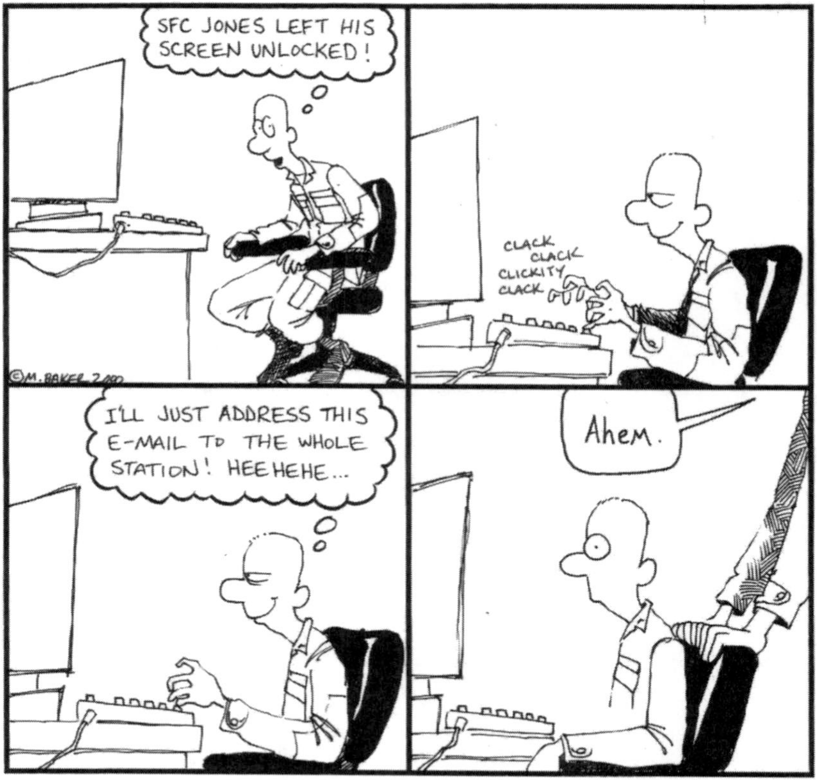
SFC JONES LEFT HIS SCREEN UNLOCKED!
©M. BAKER 2000
CLACK CLACK CLICKITY CLACK
I'LL JUST ADDRESS THIS E-MAIL TO THE WHOLE STATION! HEEHEHE...
Ahem.

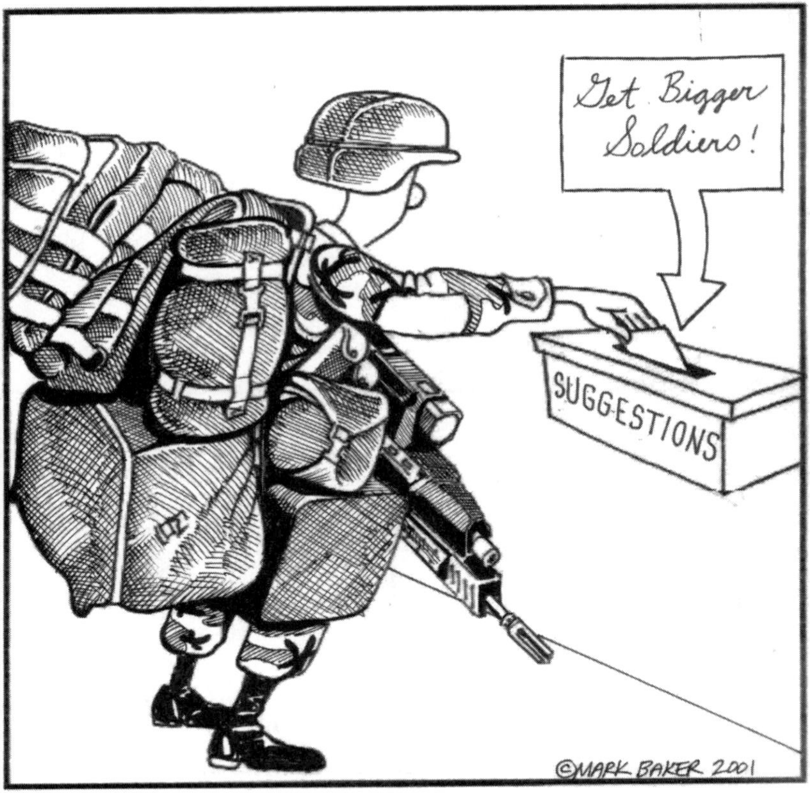
Get Bigger Soldiers!
SUGGESTIONS
©MARK BAKER 2001

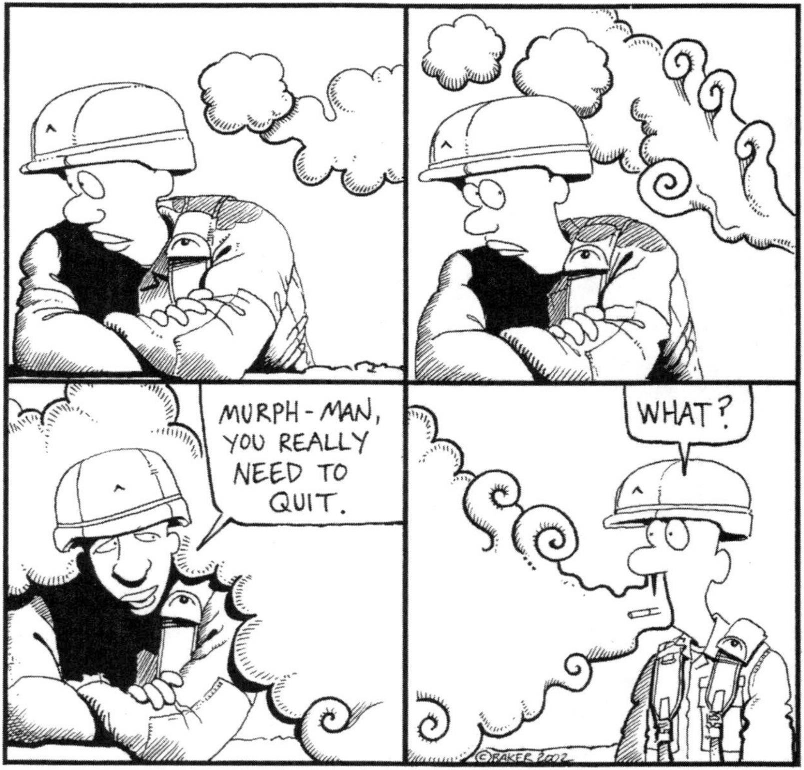
MURPH - MAN, YOU REALLY NEED TO QUIT.
WHAT?
©BAKER 2002

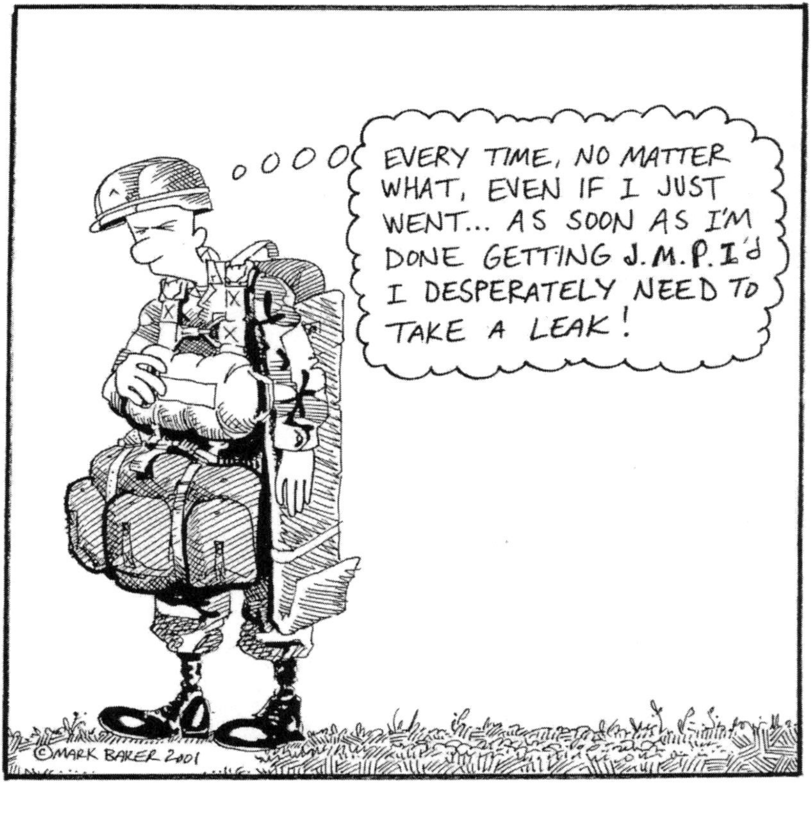
EVERY TIME, NO MATTER WHAT, EVEN IF I JUST WENT... AS SOON AS I'M DONE GETTING J.M.P.I'd I DESPERATELY NEED TO TAKE A LEAK!
©MARK BAKER 2001

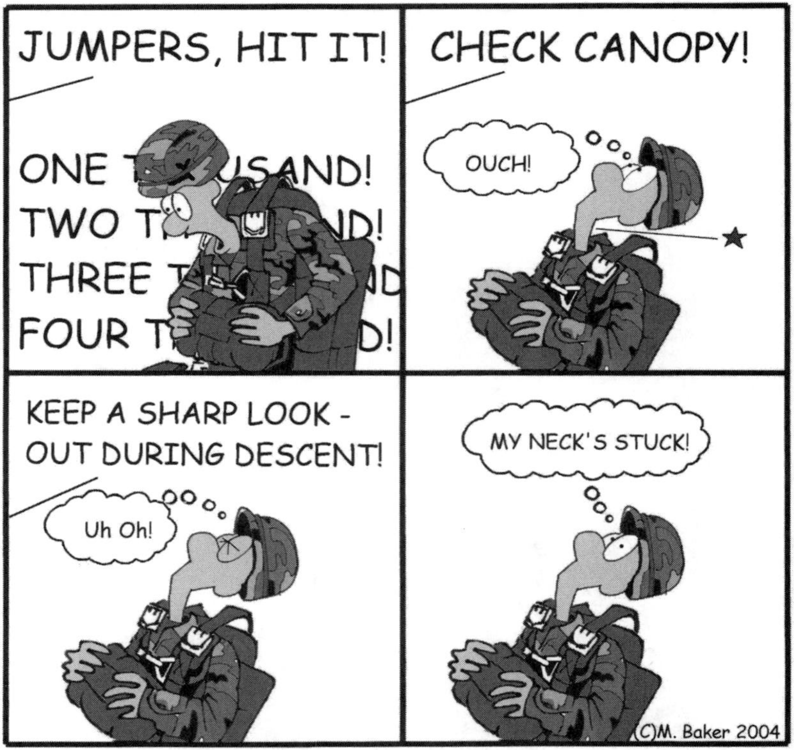
JUMPERS, HIT IT!
ONE T USAND!
TWO T ND!
THREE T ND
FOUR T D!
CHECK CANOPY!
OUCH!
KEEP A SHARP LOOK - OUT DURING DESCENT!
Uh Oh!
MY NECK'S STUCK!
(C)M. Baker 2004

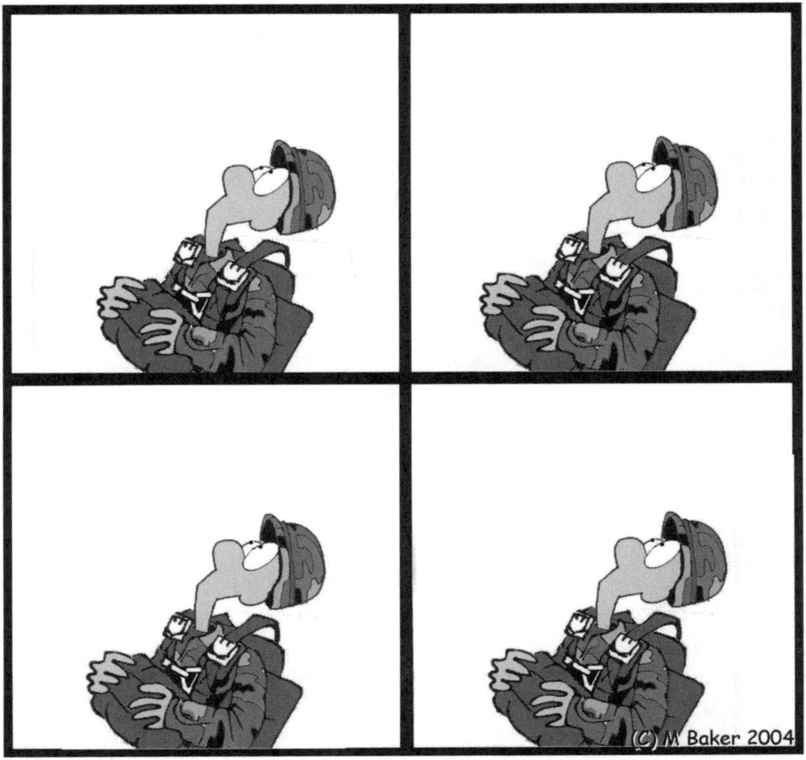
(C) M Baker 2004

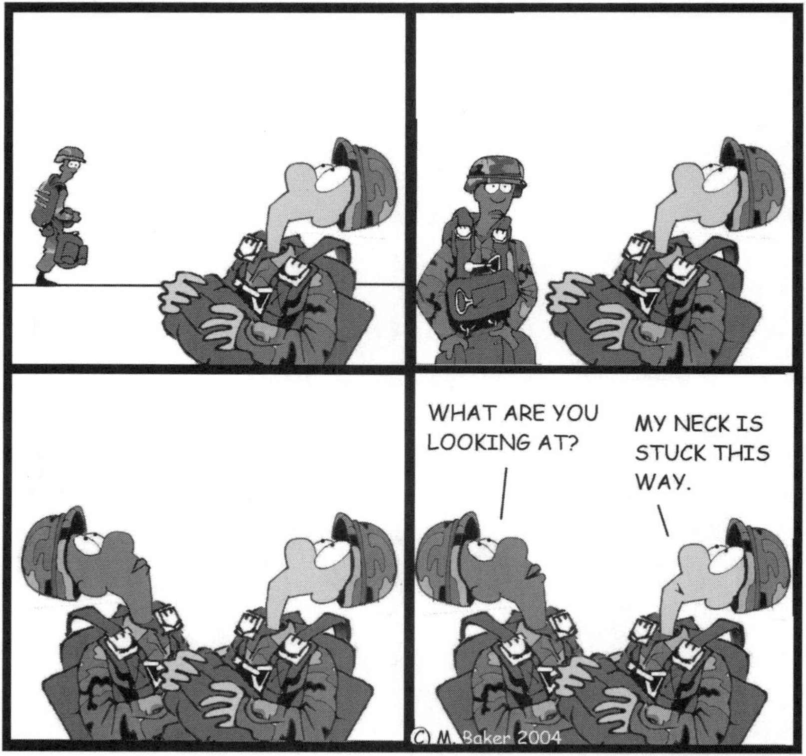
WHAT ARE YOU LOOKING AT?
MY NECK IS STUCK THIS WAY.
© M. Baker 2004

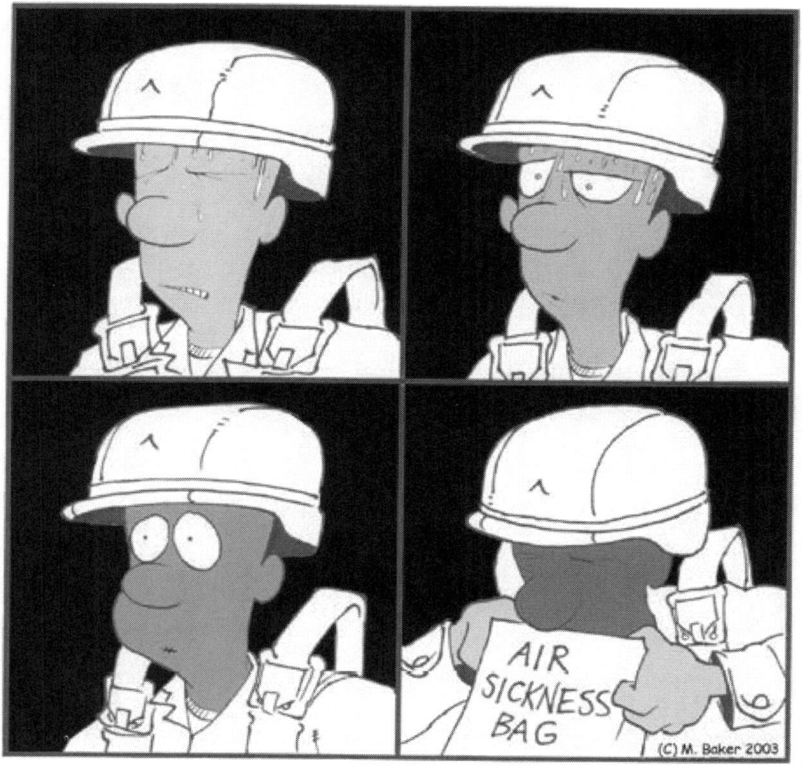
AIR
SICKNESS
BAG
(C) M. Baker 2003

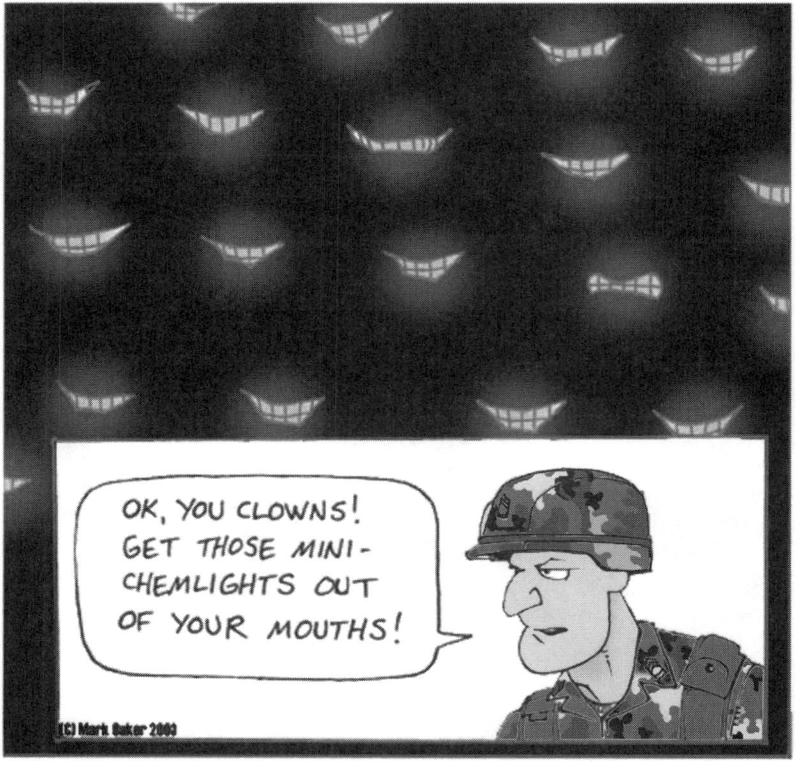
OK, YOU CLOWNS! GET THOSE MINI-CHEMLIGHTS OUT OF YOUR MOUTHS!
(C) Mark Baker 2003

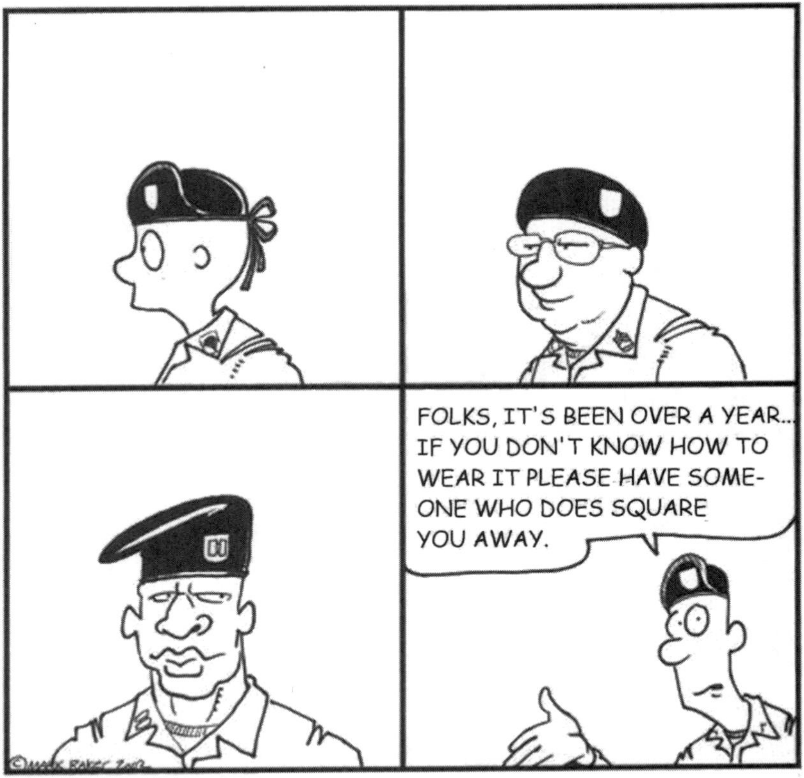
FOLKS, IT'S BEEN OVER A YEAR... IF YOU DON'T KNOW HOW TO WEAR IT PLEASE HAVE SOME-ONE WHO DOES SQUARE YOU AWAY.

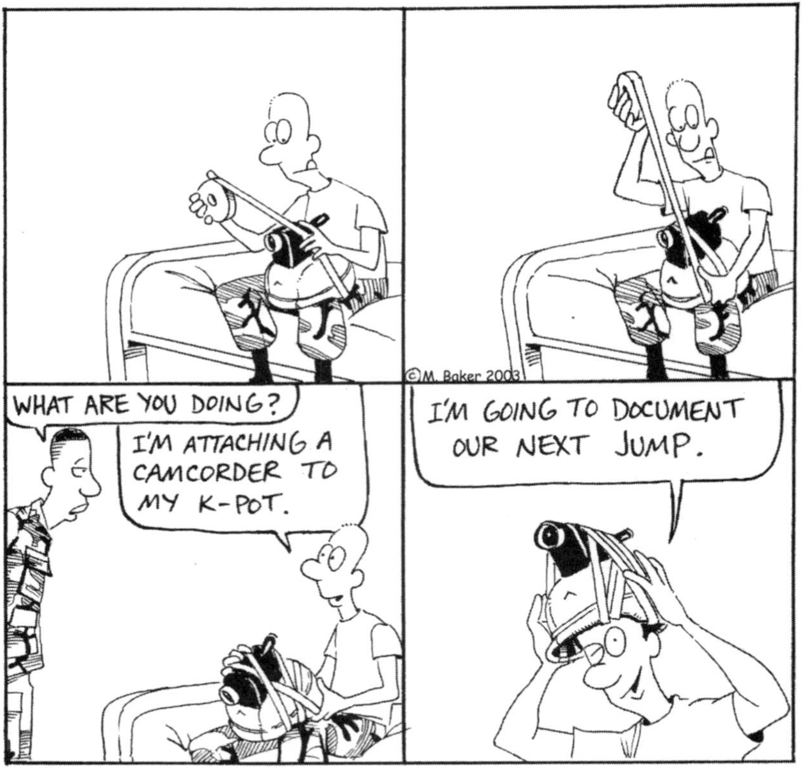
©M. Baker 2003
WHAT ARE YOU DOING?
I'M ATTACHING A CAMCORDER TO MY K-POT.
I'M GOING TO DOCUMENT OUR NEXT JUMP.

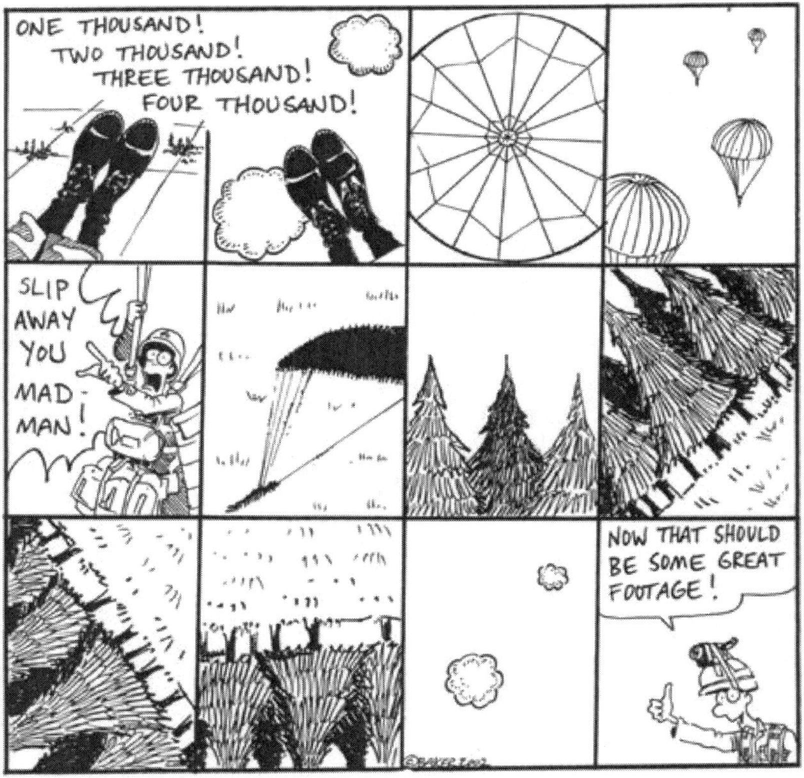
ONE THOUSAND! TWO THOUSAND! THREE THOUSAND! FOUR THOUSAND!
SLIP AWAY YOU MAD-MAN!
NOW THAT SHOULD BE SOME GREAT FOOTAGE!

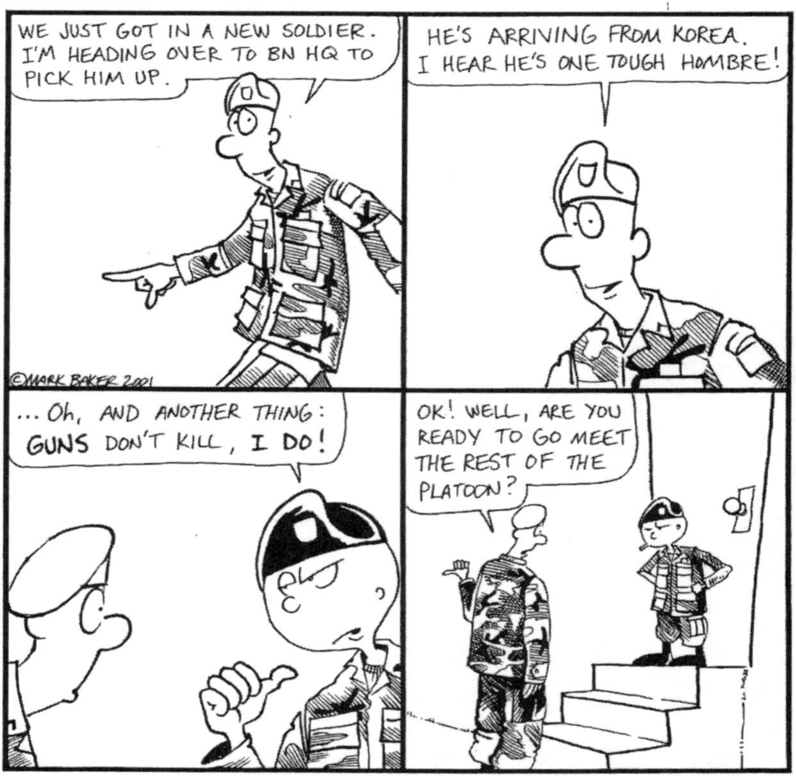
WE JUST GOT IN A NEW SOLDIER. I'M HEADING OVER TO BN HQ TO PICK HIM UP.
©MARK BAKER 2001
HE'S ARRIVING FROM KOREA. I HEAR HE'S ONE TOUGH HOMBRE!
... Oh, AND ANOTHER THING: GUNS DON'T KILL, I DO!
OK! WELL, ARE YOU READY TO GO MEET THE REST OF THE PLATOON?

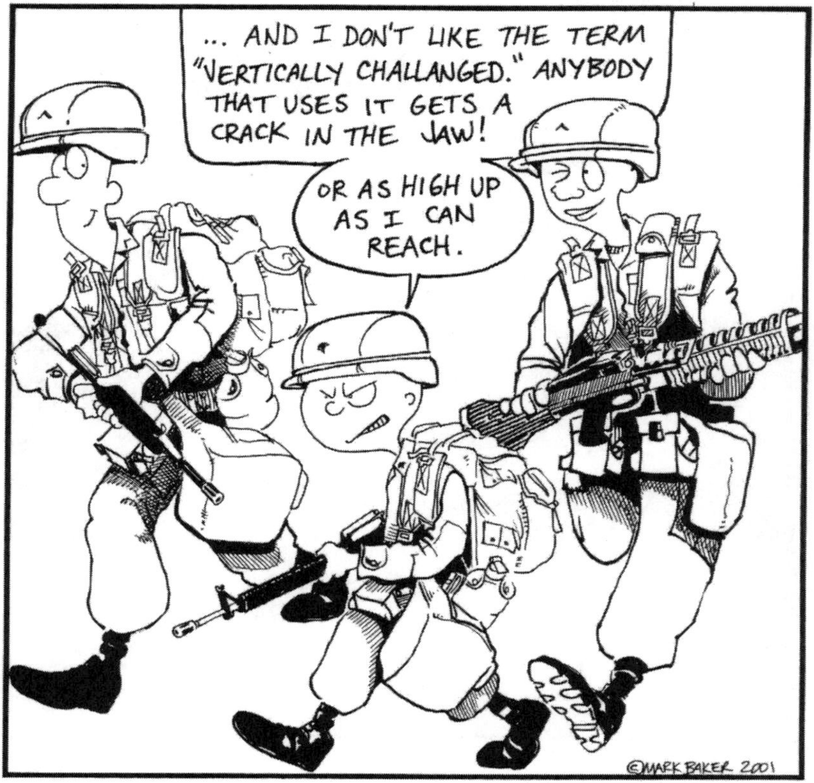
... AND I DON'T LIKE THE TERM "VERTICALLY CHALLANGED." ANYBODY THAT USES IT GETS A CRACK IN THE JAW!
OR AS HIGH UP AS I CAN REACH.
©MARK BAKER 2001

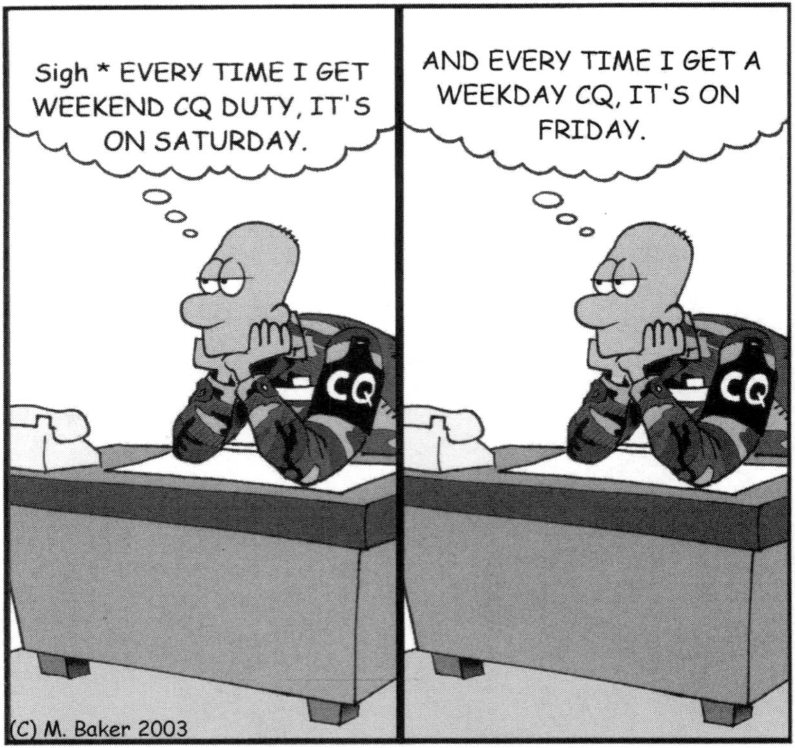
Sigh * EVERY TIME I GET WEEKEND CQ DUTY, IT'S ON SATURDAY.
CQ
(C) M. Baker 2003
AND EVERY TIME I GET A WEEKDAY CQ, IT'S ON FRIDAY.
CQ

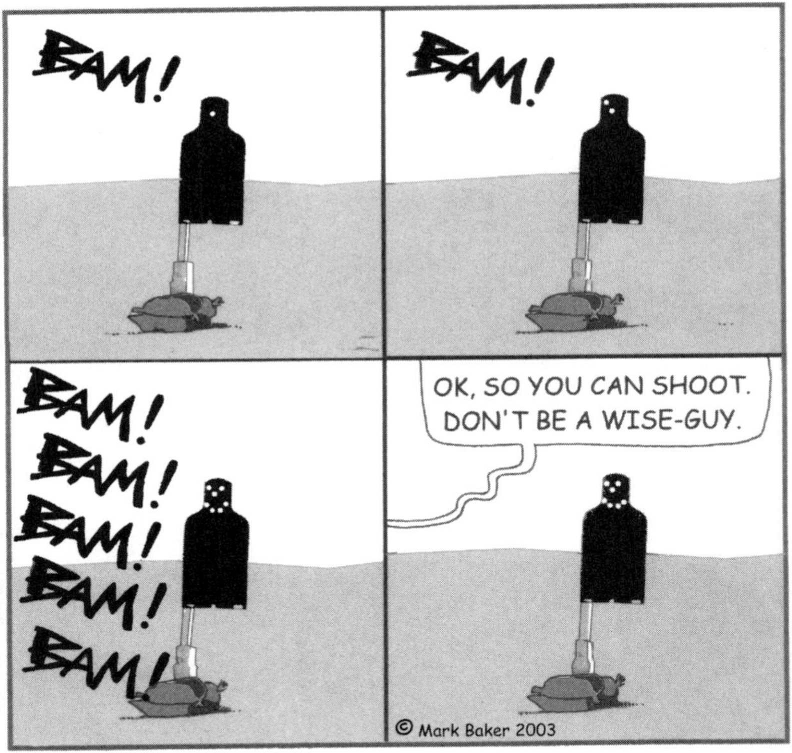
BAM!
BAM!
BAM!
BAM!
BAM!
BAM!
BAM!
OK, SO YOU CAN SHOOT.
DON'T BE A WISE-GUY.
© Mark Baker 2003

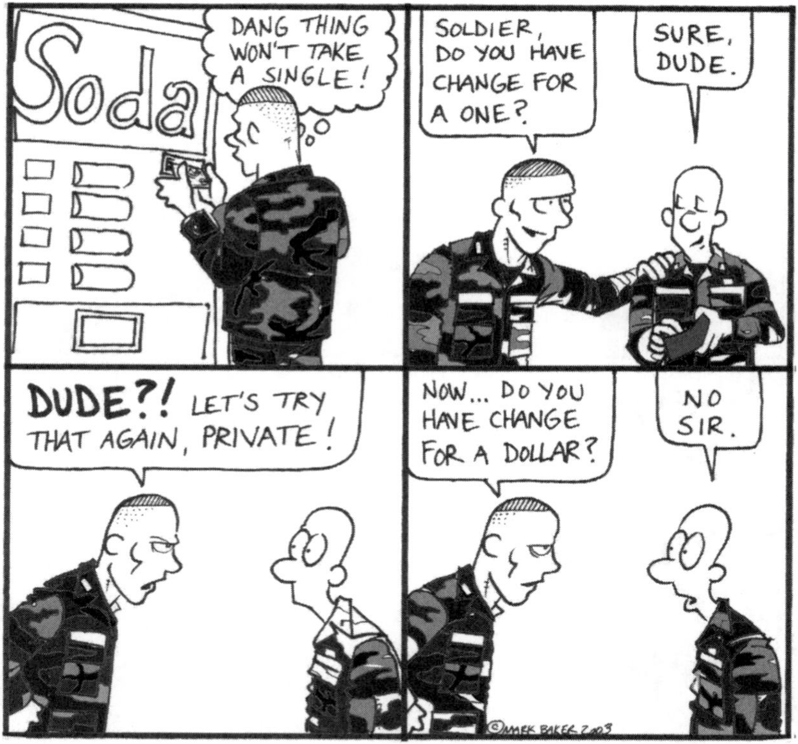

Soda
DANG THING WON'T TAKE A SINGLE!
SOLDIER, DO YOU HAVE CHANGE FOR A ONE?
SURE, DUDE.
DUDE?! LET'S TRY THAT AGAIN, PRIVATE!
NOW... DO YOU HAVE CHANGE FOR A DOLLAR?
NO SIR.

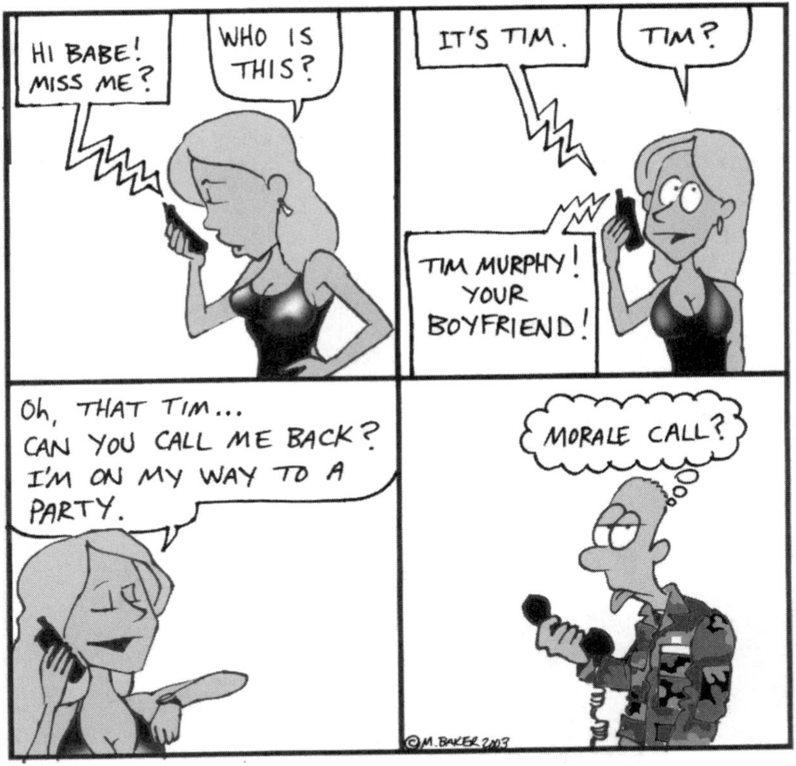
HI BABE! MISS ME?
WHO IS THIS?
IT'S TIM.
TIM?
TIM MURPHY! YOUR BOYFRIEND!
Oh, THAT TIM... CAN YOU CALL ME BACK? I'M ON MY WAY TO A PARTY.
MORALE CALL?
©M. BAKER 2003

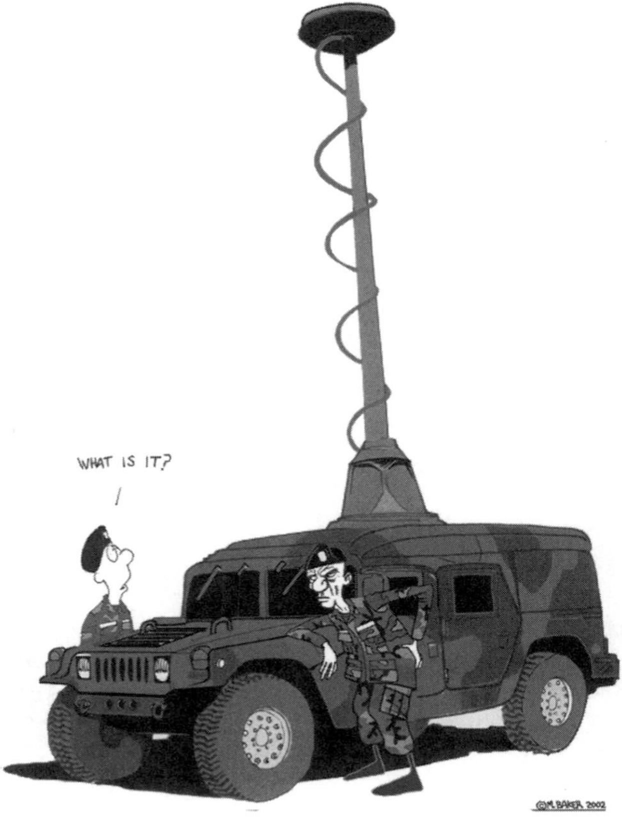
WHAT IS IT?
©M. BAKER 2002

From an E-mail: "Mark, my thoughts exactly, what is it?"

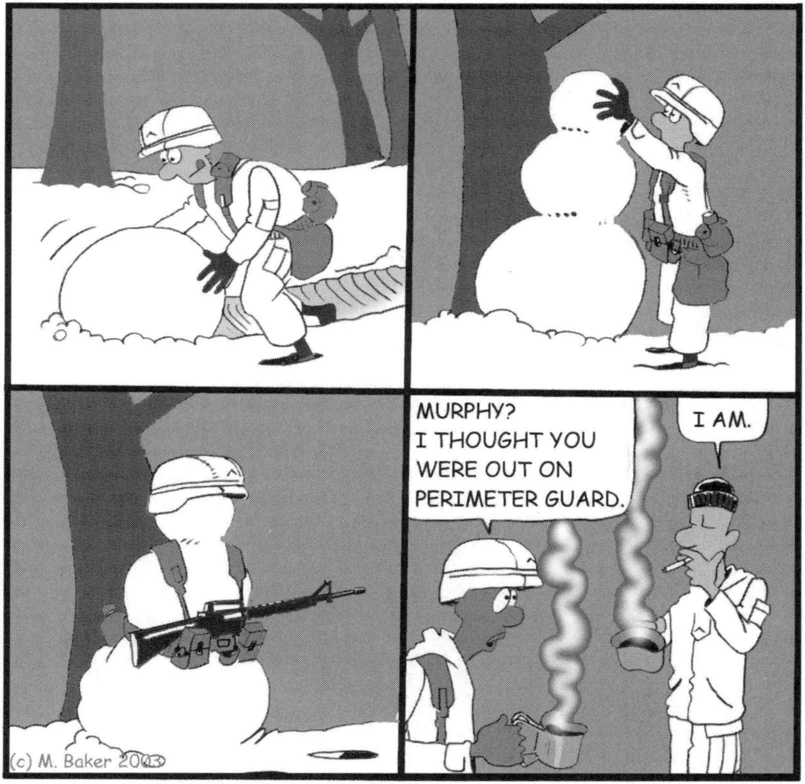
MURPHY?
I THOUGHT YOU
WERE OUT ON
PERIMETER GUARD.
I AM.
(c) M. Baker 2003

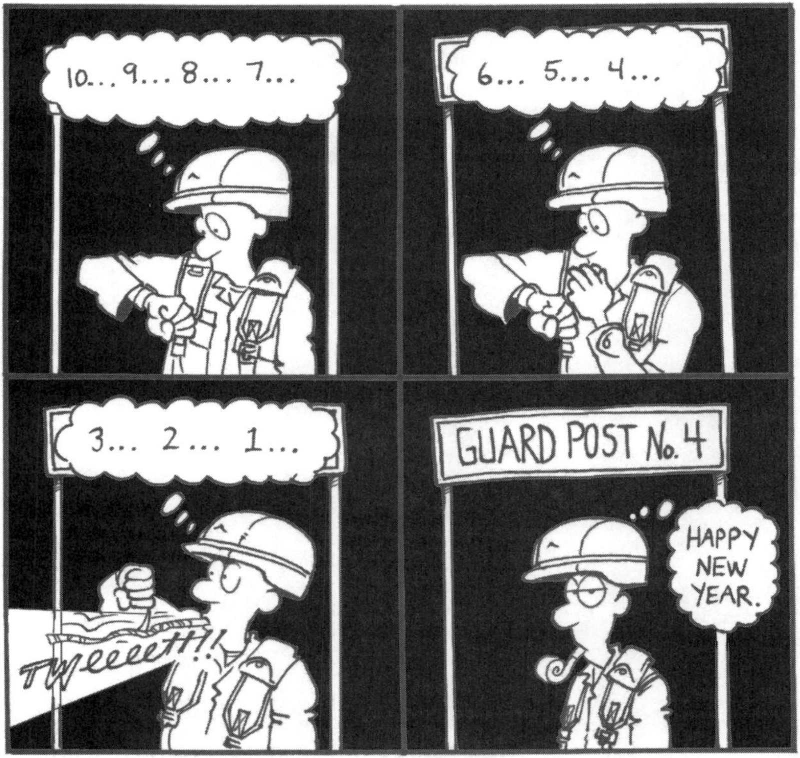
10... 9... 8... 7...
6... 5... 4...
3... 2... 1...
TWEEEEETT!!
GUARD POST No. 4
HAPPY NEW YEAR.

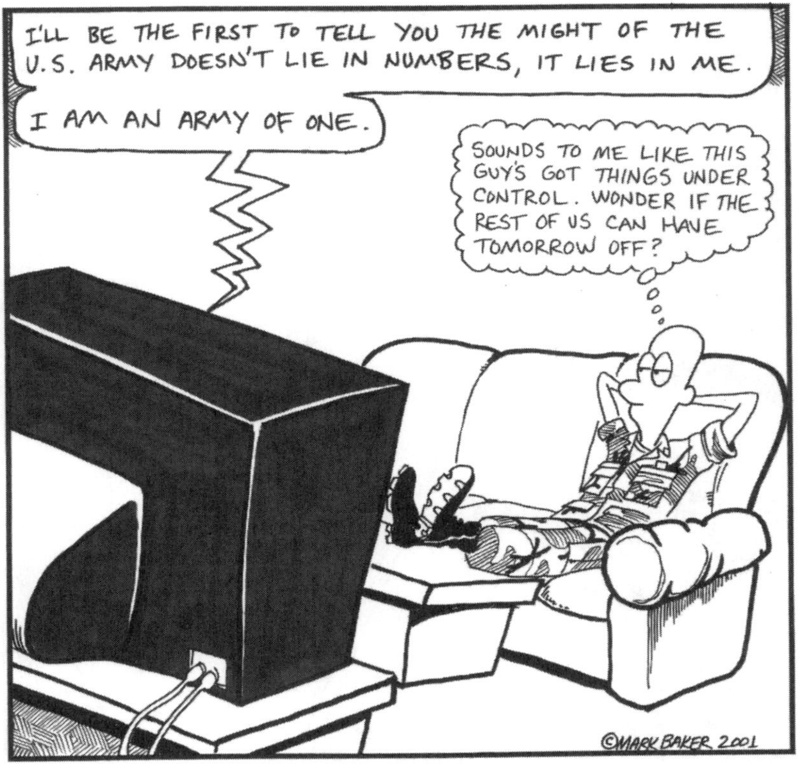
I'LL BE THE FIRST TO TELL YOU THE MIGHT OF THE U.S. ARMY DOESN'T LIE IN NUMBERS, IT LIES IN ME.
I AM AN ARMY OF ONE.
SOUNDS TO ME LIKE THIS GUY'S GOT THINGS UNDER CONTROL. WONDER IF THE REST OF US CAN HAVE TOMORROW OFF?
©MARK BAKER 2001

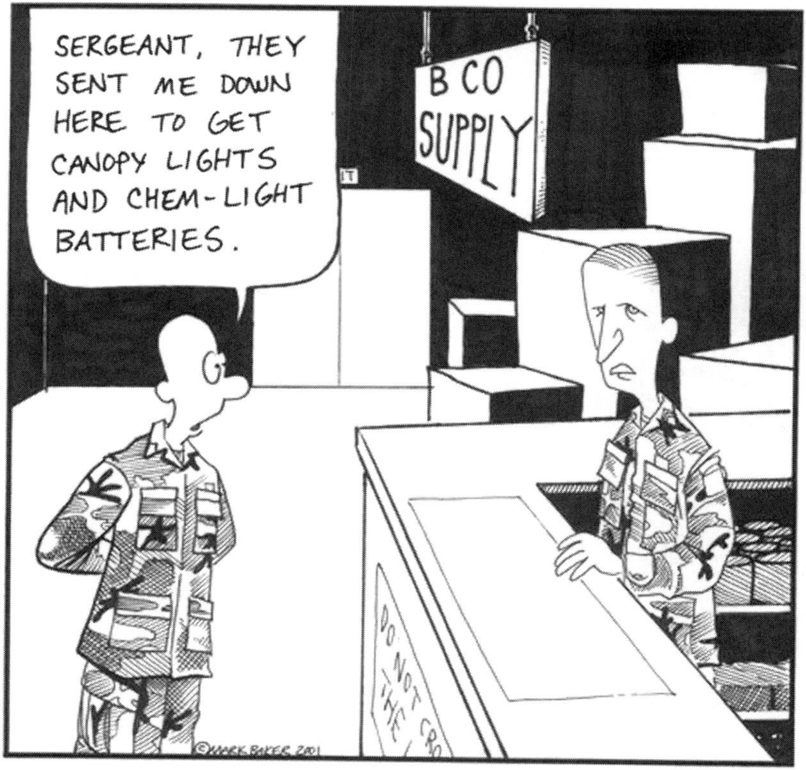
SERGEANT, THEY SENT ME DOWN HERE TO GET CANOPY LIGHTS AND CHEM-LIGHT BATTERIES.
B CO SUPPLY

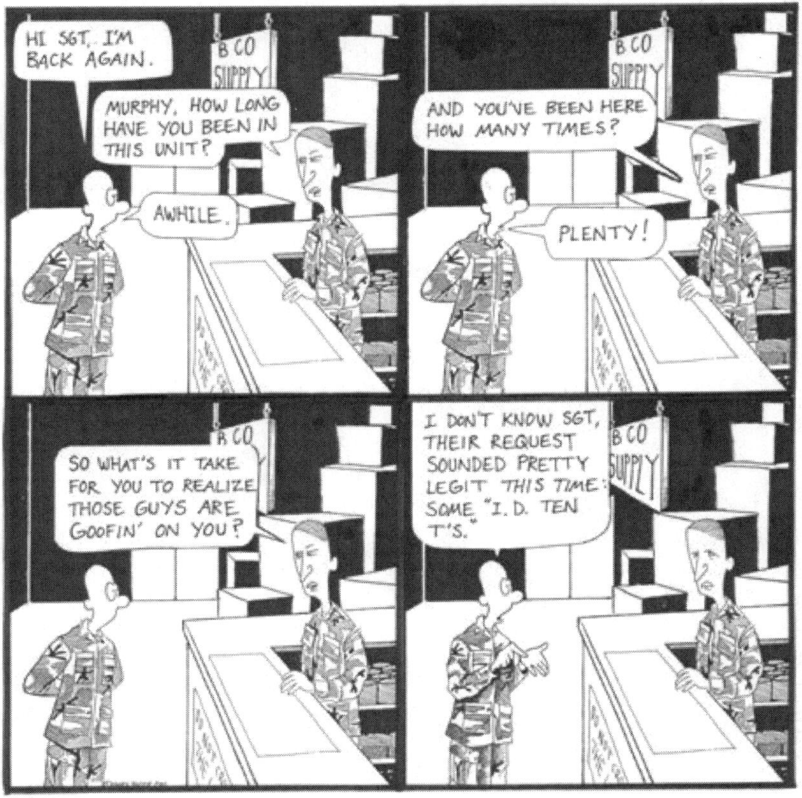
HI SGT, I'M BACK AGAIN.
B CO SUPPLY
MURPHY, HOW LONG HAVE YOU BEEN IN THIS UNIT?
AWHILE.
AND YOU'VE BEEN HERE HOW MANY TIMES?
PLENTY!
SO WHAT'S IT TAKE FOR YOU TO REALIZE THOSE GUYS ARE GOOFIN' ON YOU?
I DON'T KNOW SGT, THEIR REQUEST SOUNDED PRETTY LEGIT THIS TIME: SOME "I. D. TEN T'S."

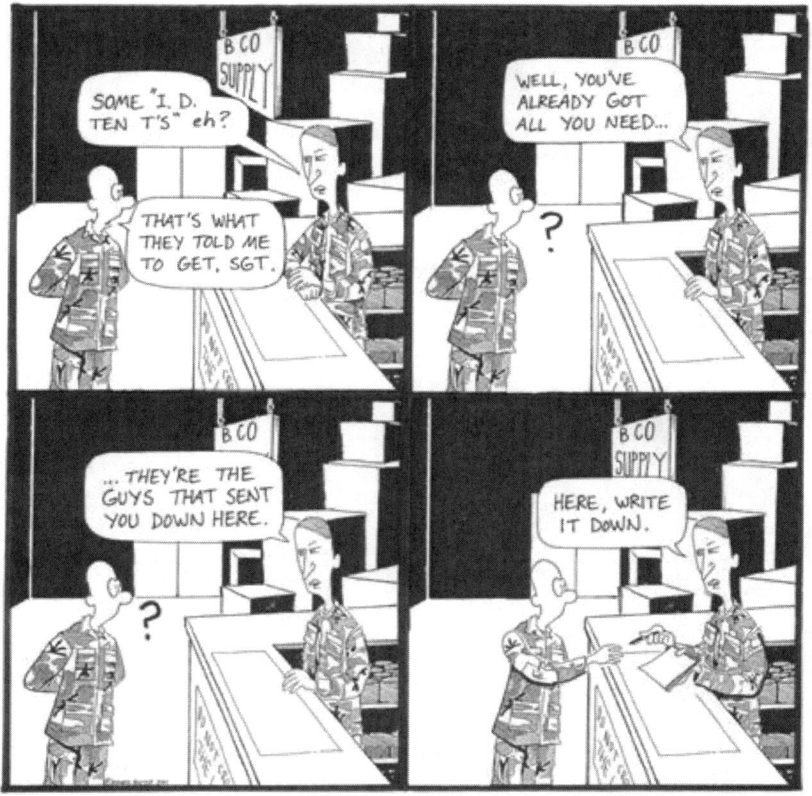
B CO
SUPPLY
SOME "I. D. TEN T'S" eh?
THAT'S WHAT THEY TOLD ME TO GET, SGT.
B CO
WELL, YOU'VE ALREADY GOT ALL YOU NEED...
?
B CO
... THEY'RE THE GUYS THAT SENT YOU DOWN HERE.
?
B CO
SUPPLY
HERE, WRITE IT DOWN.

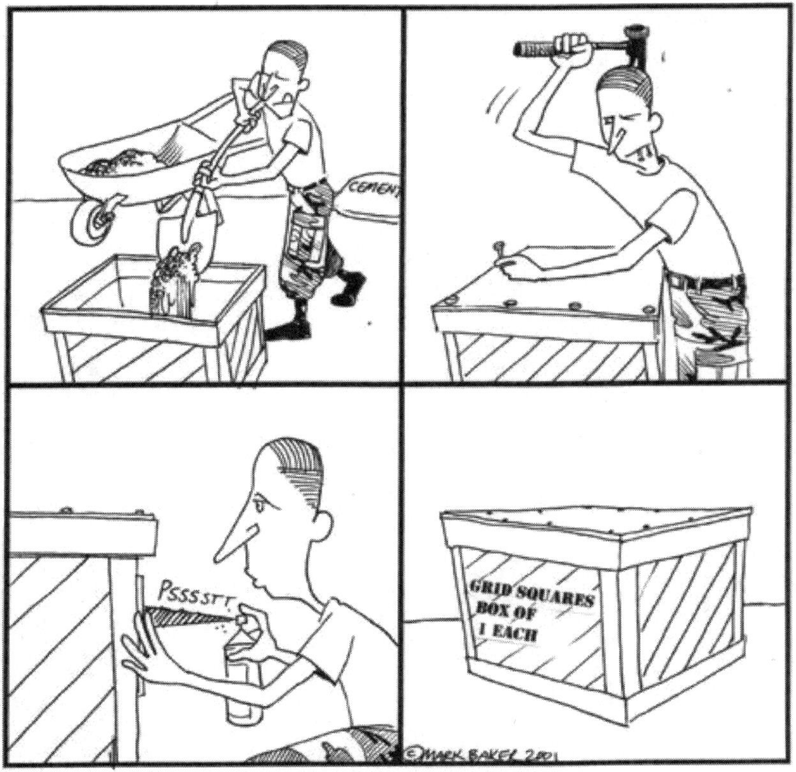
CEMENT
PSSSSTT
GRID SQUARES
BOX OF
1 EACH
©MARK BAKER 2001

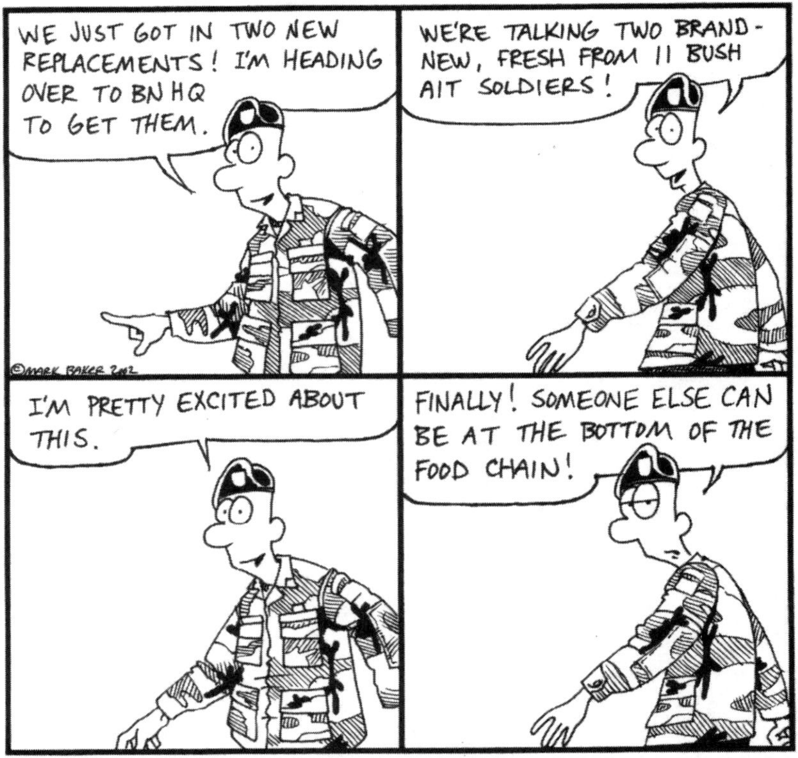
WE JUST GOT IN TWO NEW REPLACEMENTS! I'M HEADING OVER TO BN HQ TO GET THEM.
©MARK BAKER 2002
WE'RE TALKING TWO BRAND-NEW, FRESH FROM 11 BUSH AIT SOLDIERS!
I'M PRETTY EXCITED ABOUT THIS.
FINALLY! SOMEONE ELSE CAN BE AT THE BOTTOM OF THE FOOD CHAIN!

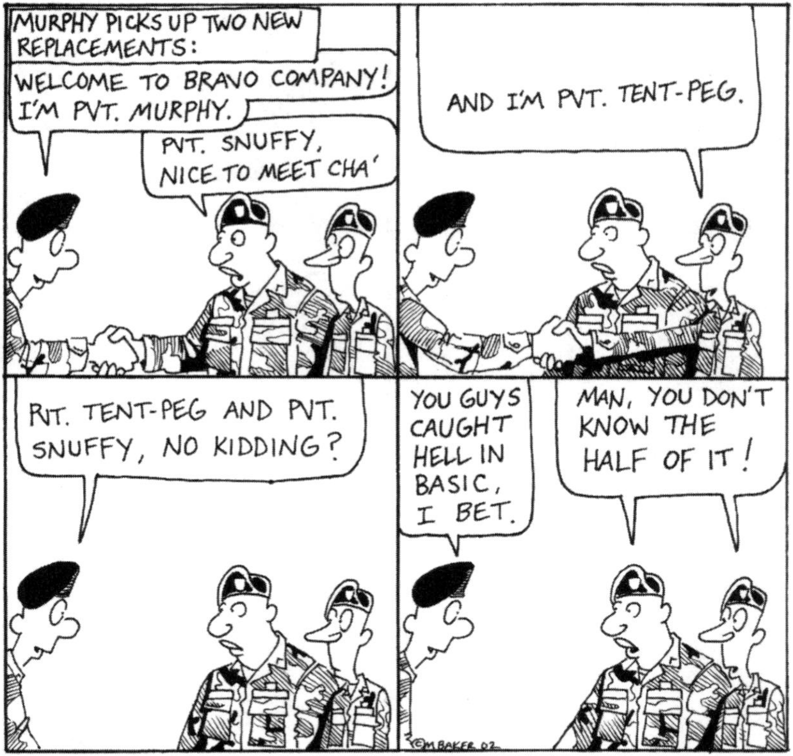
MURPHY PICKS UP TWO NEW REPLACEMENTS:
WELCOME TO BRAVO COMPANY! I'M PVT. MURPHY.
PVT. SNUFFY, NICE TO MEET CHA'
AND I'M PVT. TENT-PEG.
PVT. TENT-PEG AND PVT. SNUFFY, NO KIDDING?
YOU GUYS CAUGHT HELL IN BASIC, I BET.
MAN, YOU DON'T KNOW THE HALF OF IT!
©M BAKER 02

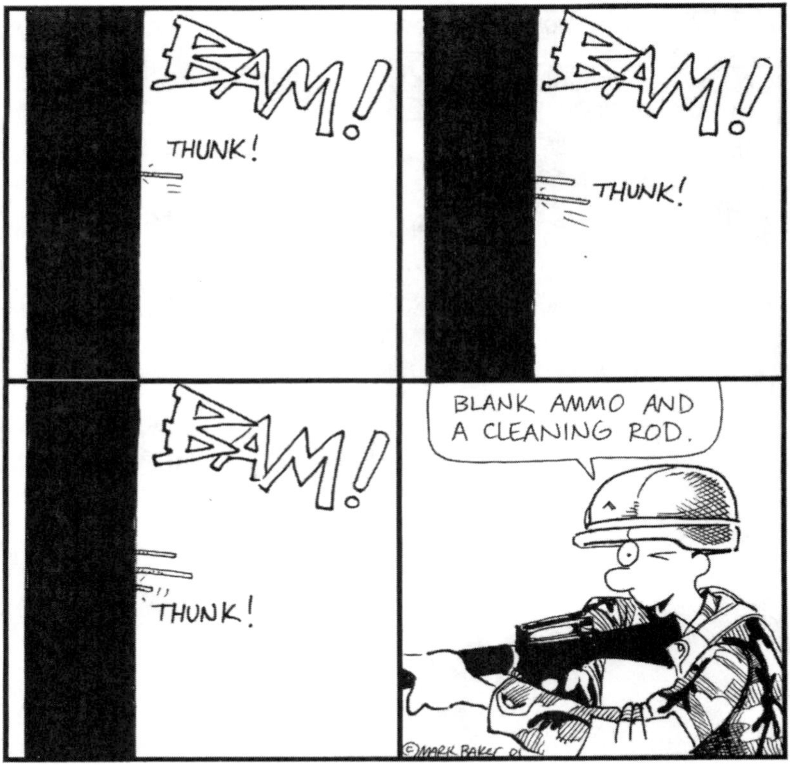
BAM!
THUNK!
BAM!
THUNK!
BAM!
THUNK!
BLANK AMMO AND A CLEANING ROD.
©MARK BAKER

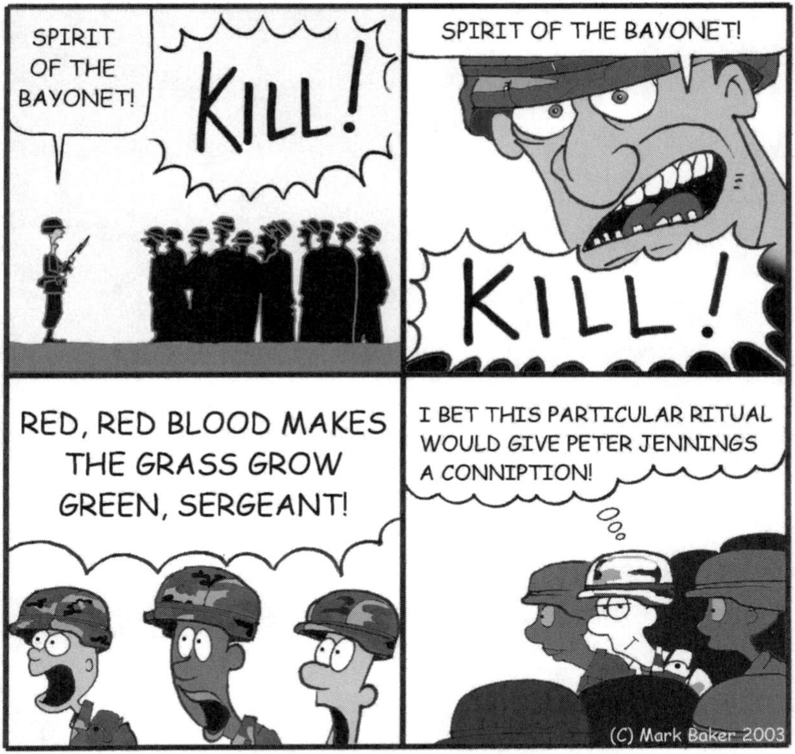
SPIRIT OF THE BAYONET!
KILL!
SPIRIT OF THE BAYONET!
KILL!
RED, RED BLOOD MAKES THE GRASS GROW GREEN, SERGEANT!
I BET THIS PARTICULAR RITUAL WOULD GIVE PETER JENNINGS A CONNIPTION!
(C) Mark Baker 2003

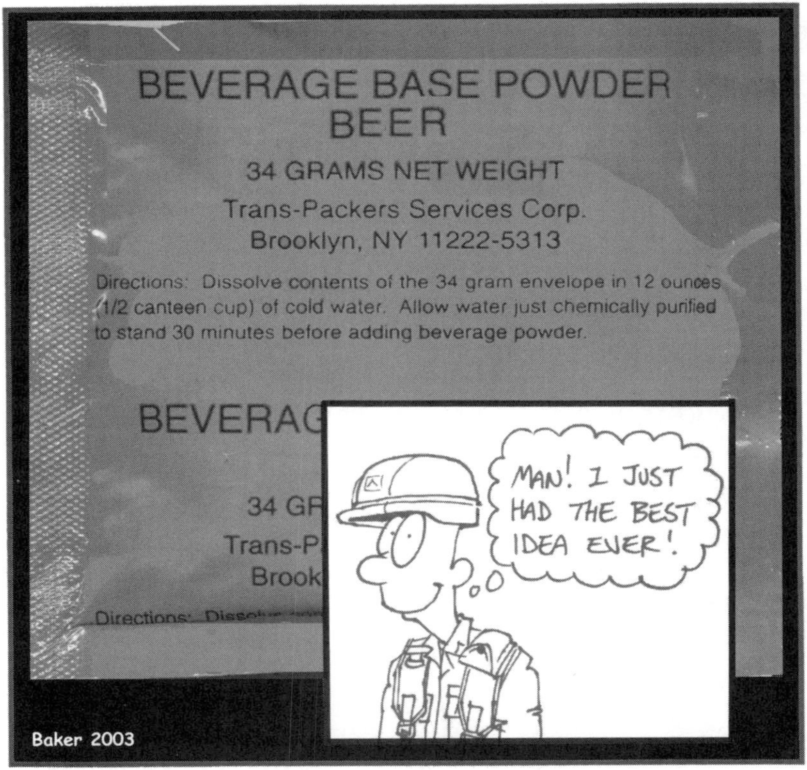
BEVERAGE BASE POWDER
BEER
34 GRAMS NET WEIGHT
Trans-Packers Services Corp.
Brooklyn, NY 11222-5313
Directions: Dissolve contents of the 34 gram envelope in 12 ounces (1/2 canteen cup) of cold water. Allow water just chemically purified to stand 30 minutes before adding beverage powder.
BEVERAG
34 GR
Trans-P
Brook
MAN! I JUST HAD THE BEST IDEA EVER!
Baker 2003

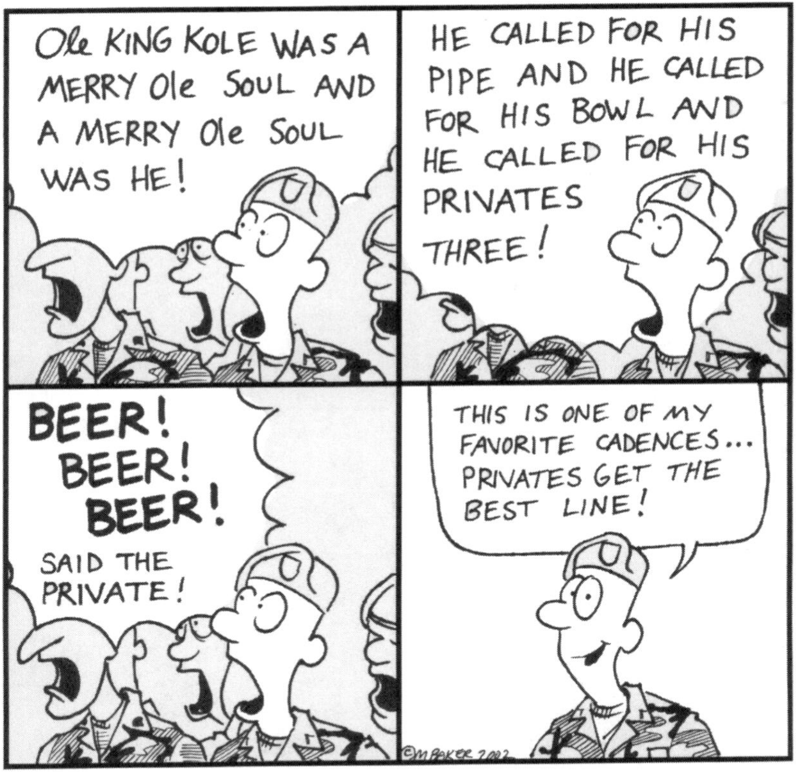
Ole KING KOLE WAS A MERRY Ole SOUL AND A MERRY Ole SOUL WAS HE!
HE CALLED FOR HIS PIPE AND HE CALLED FOR HIS BOWL AND HE CALLED FOR HIS PRIVATES THREE!
BEER! BEER! BEER!
SAID THE PRIVATE!
THIS IS ONE OF MY FAVORITE CADENCES... PRIVATES GET THE BEST LINE!
©M BAKER 2002

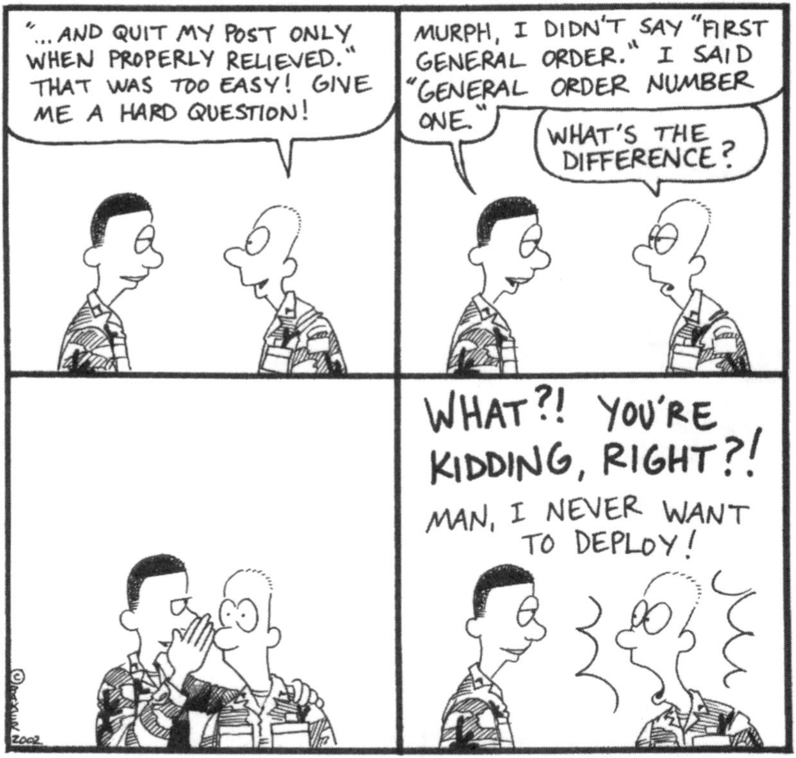
"... AND QUIT MY POST ONLY WHEN PROPERLY RELIEVED." THAT WAS TOO EASY! GIVE ME A HARD QUESTION!
MURPH, I DIDN'T SAY "FIRST GENERAL ORDER." I SAID "GENERAL ORDER NUMBER ONE."
WHAT'S THE DIFFERENCE?
WHAT?! YOU'RE KIDDING, RIGHT?!
MAN, I NEVER WANT TO DEPLOY!
©
2002

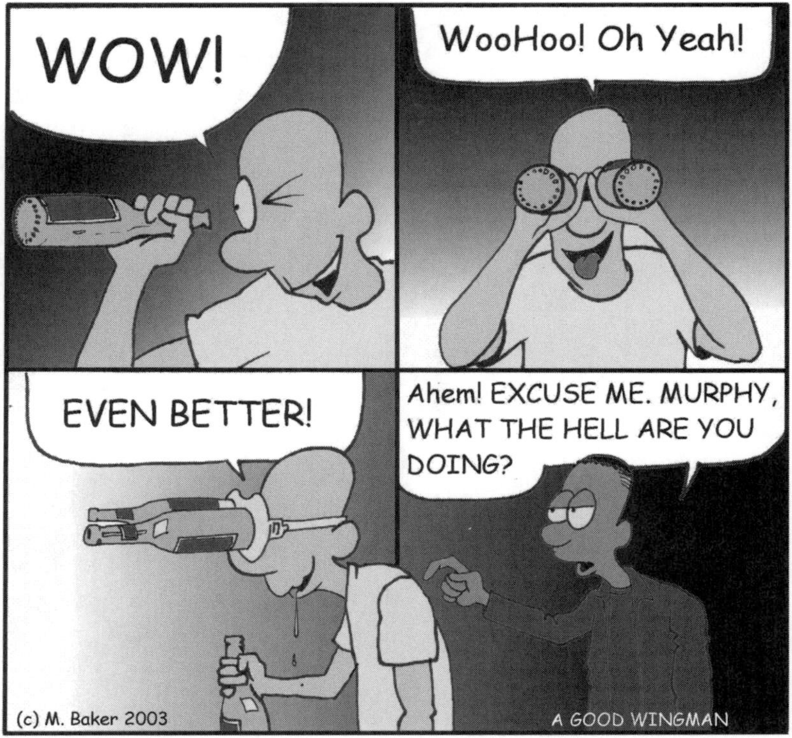
WOW!
WooHoo! Oh Yeah!
EVEN BETTER!
Ahem! EXCUSE ME. MURPHY, WHAT THE HELL ARE YOU DOING?
(c) M. Baker 2003
A GOOD WINGMAN

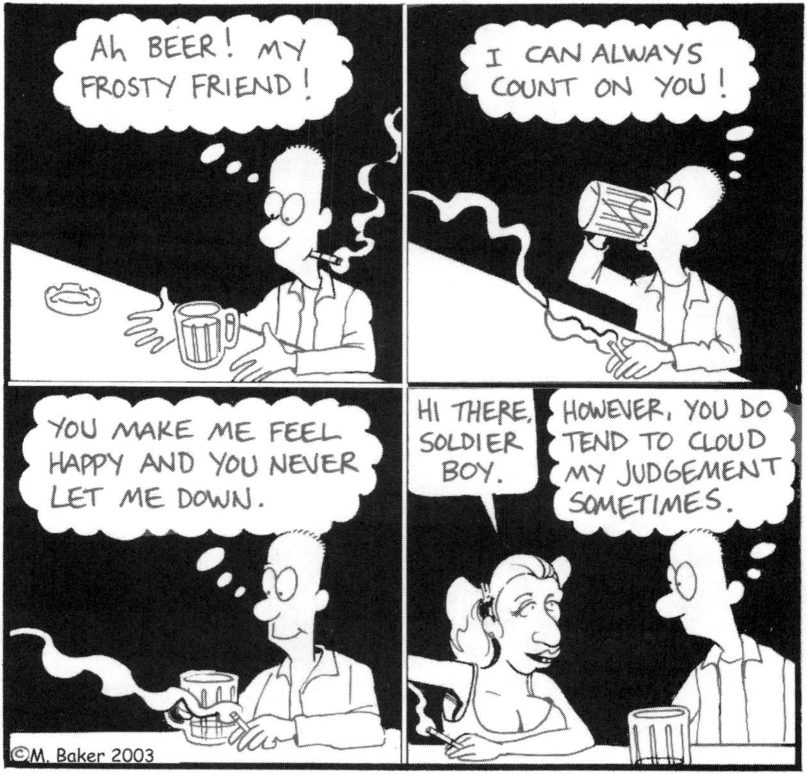
AH BEER! MY FROSTY FRIEND!
I CAN ALWAYS COUNT ON YOU!
YOU MAKE ME FEEL HAPPY AND YOU NEVER LET ME DOWN.
HI THERE, SOLDIER BOY.
HOWEVER, YOU DO TEND TO CLOUD MY JUDGEMENT SOMETIMES.
©M. Baker 2003

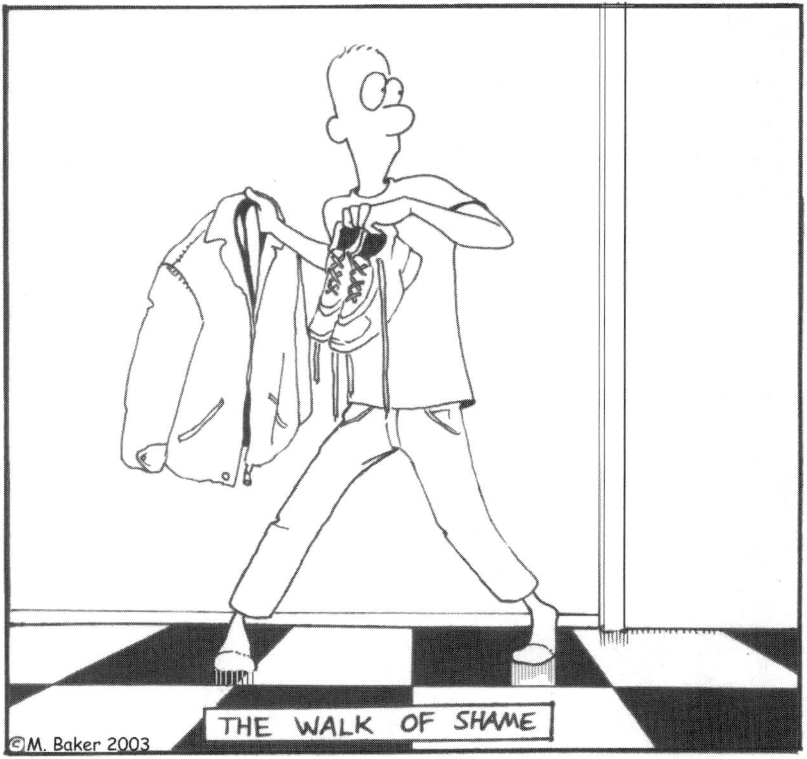
THE WALK OF SHAME
©M. Baker 2003

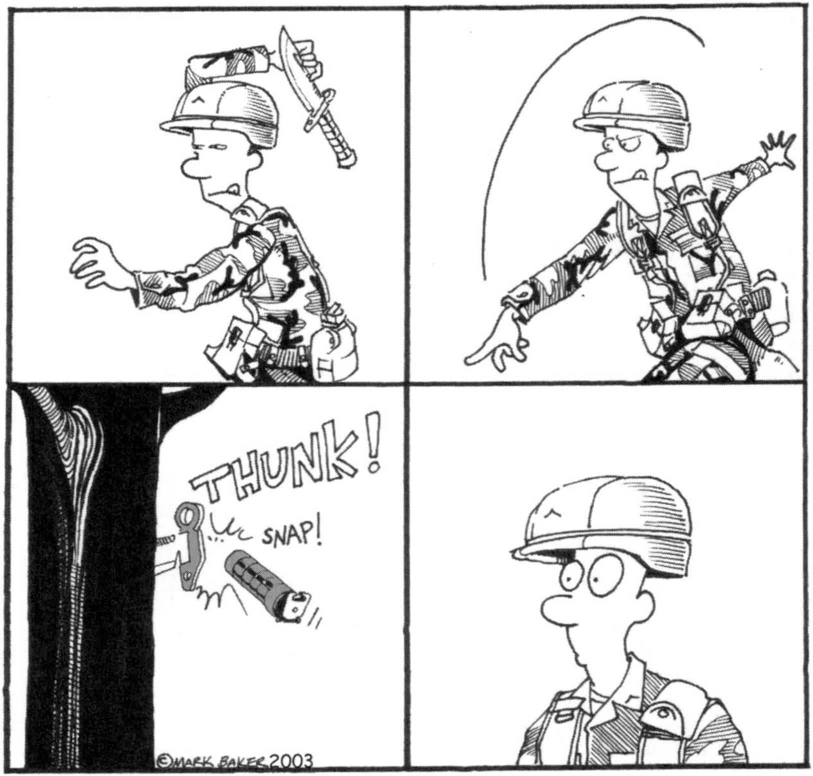
THUNK!
SNAP!
©MARK BAKER 2003

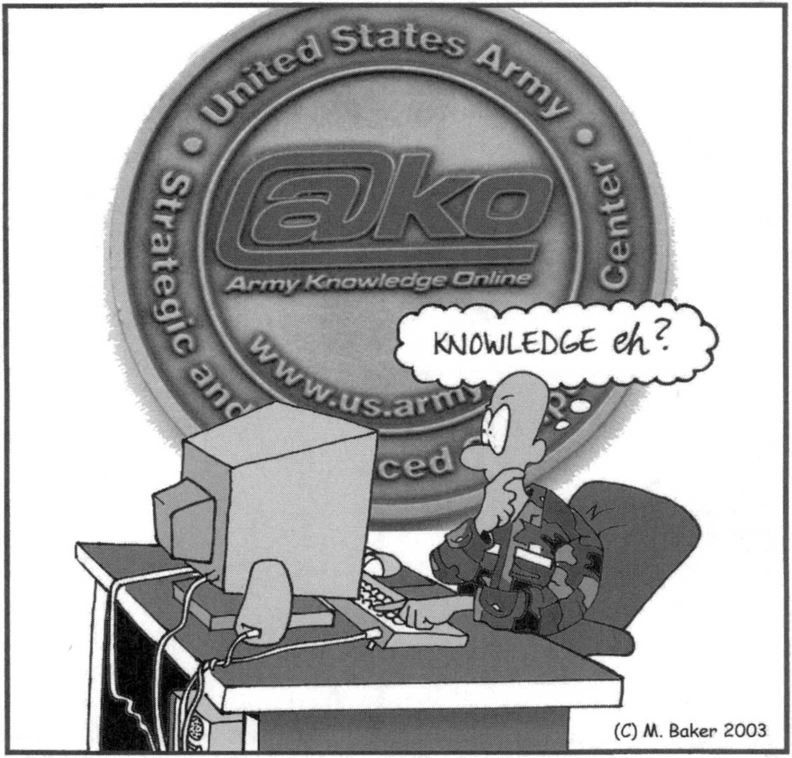
United States Army
Strategic
Center
ako
Army Knowledge Online
KNOWLEDGE eh?
(C) M. Baker 2003

I drew this cartoon to help promote AKO.

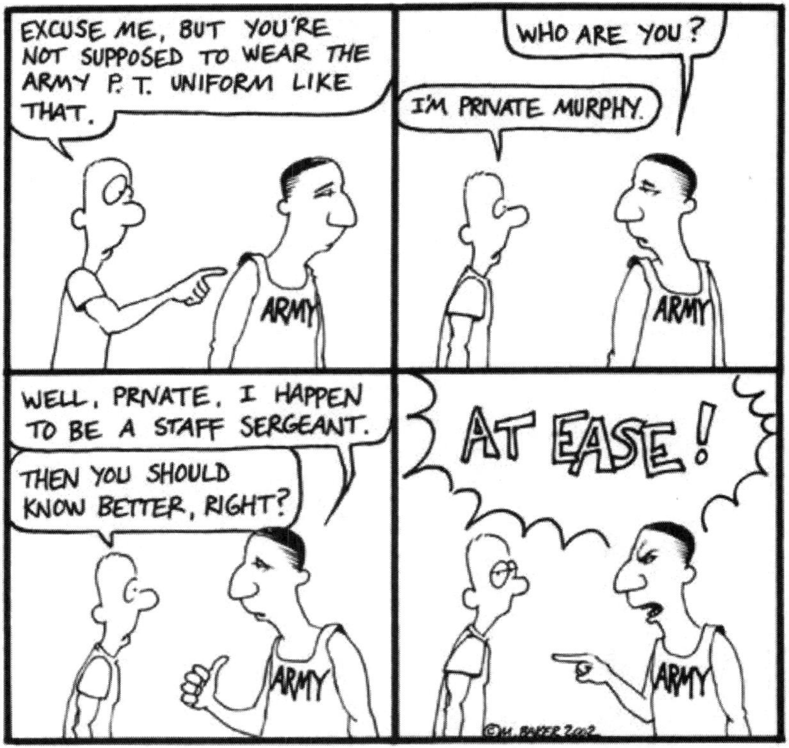
EXCUSE ME, BUT YOU'RE NOT SUPPOSED TO WEAR THE ARMY P. T. UNIFORM LIKE THAT.
ARMY
WHO ARE YOU?
I'M PRIVATE MURPHY.
ARMY
WELL, PRIVATE, I HAPPEN TO BE A STAFF SERGEANT.
THEN YOU SHOULD KNOW BETTER, RIGHT?
ARMY
AT EASE!
ARMY

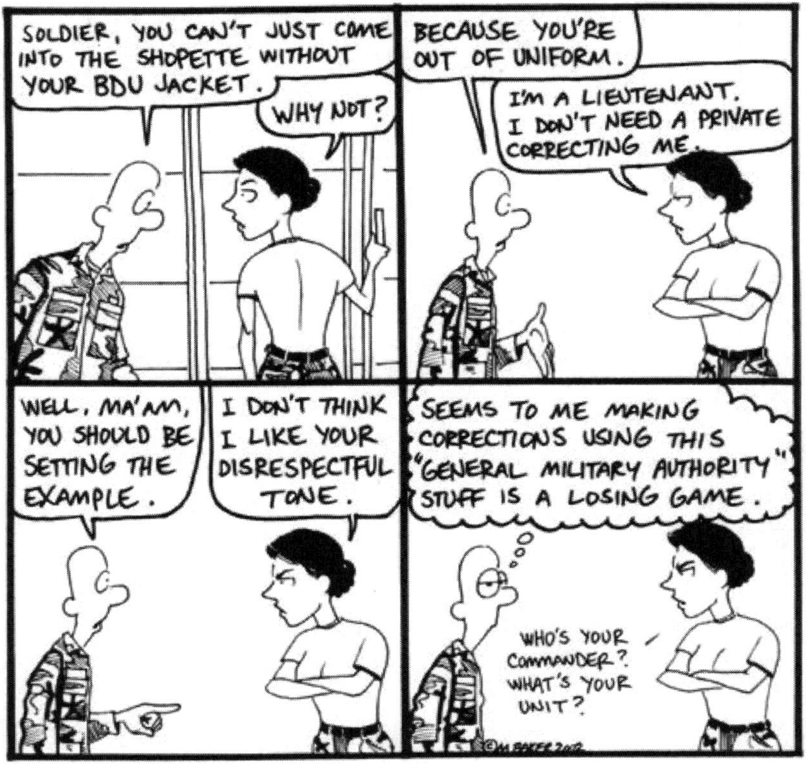
SOLDIER, YOU CAN'T JUST COME INTO THE SHOPETTE WITHOUT YOUR BDU JACKET.
WHY NOT?
BECAUSE YOU'RE OUT OF UNIFORM.
I'M A LIEUTENANT. I DON'T NEED A PRIVATE CORRECTING ME.
WELL, MA'AM, YOU SHOULD BE SETTING THE EXAMPLE.
I DON'T THINK I LIKE YOUR DISRESPECTFUL TONE.
SEEMS TO ME MAKING CORRECTIONS USING THIS "GENERAL MILITARY AUTHORITY" STUFF IS A LOSING GAME.
WHO'S YOUR COMMANDER? WHAT'S YOUR UNIT?
©M BAKER 2002

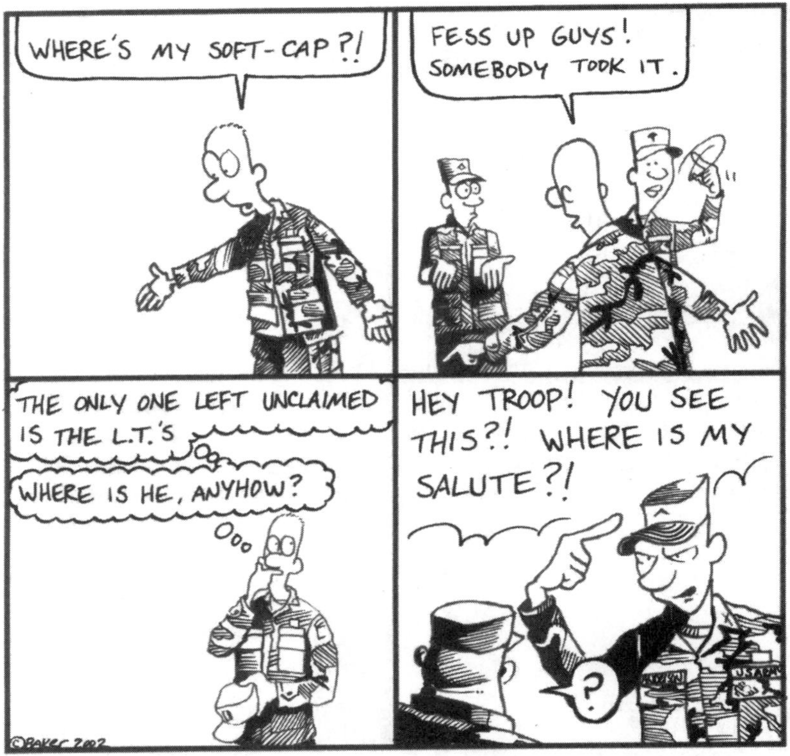
WHERE'S MY SOFT-CAP?!
FESS UP GUYS! SOMEBODY TOOK IT.
THE ONLY ONE LEFT UNCLAIMED IS THE L.T.'S
WHERE IS HE, ANYHOW?
HEY TROOP! YOU SEE THIS?! WHERE IS MY SALUTE?!
?
©BAKER 2002

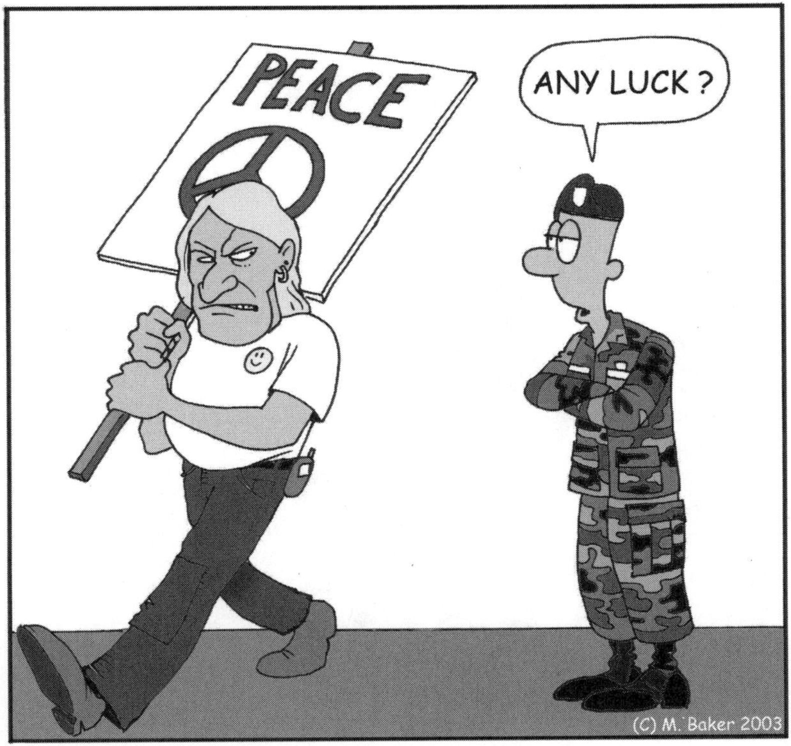
PEACE
ANY LUCK ?
(C) M. Baker 2003

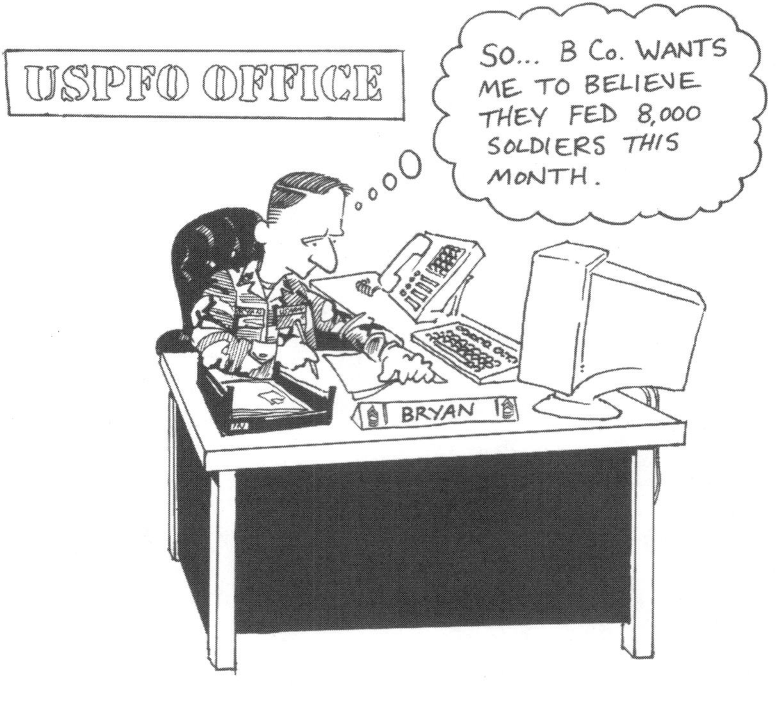
USPFO OFFICE
SO... B Co. WANTS ME TO BELIEVE THEY FED 8,000 SOLDIERS THIS MONTH.
BRYAN
MARK BAKER 2002

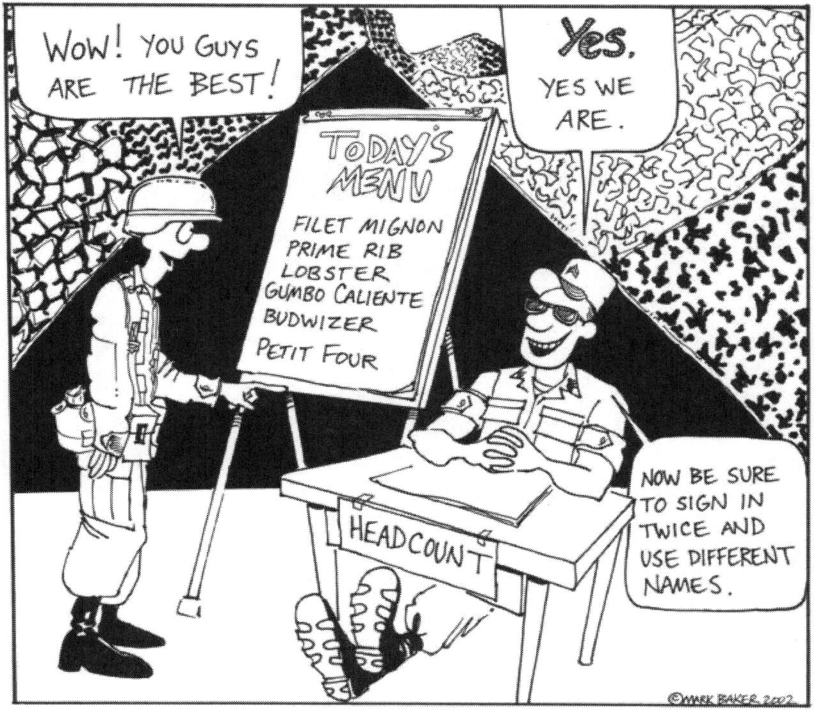
WOW! YOU GUYS ARE THE BEST!
Yes.
YES WE ARE.
TODAY'S MENU
FILET MIGNON
PRIME RIB
LOBSTER
GUMBO CALIENTE
BUDWIZER
PETIT FOUR
HEADCOUNT
NOW BE SURE TO SIGN IN TWICE AND USE DIFFERENT NAMES.
©MARK BAKER 2002

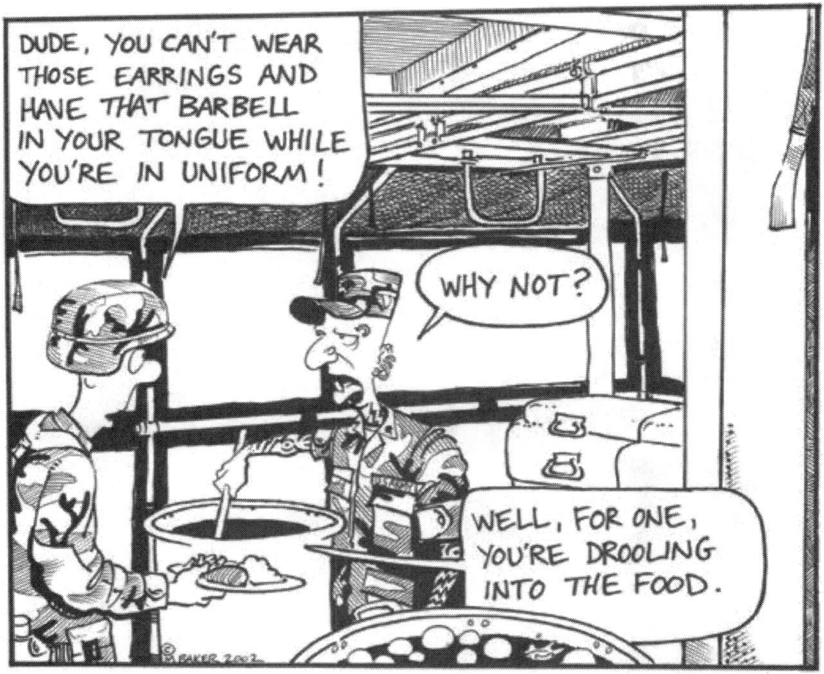
DUDE, YOU CAN'T WEAR THOSE EARRINGS AND HAVE THAT BARBELL IN YOUR TONGUE WHILE YOU'RE IN UNIFORM!
WHY NOT?
WELL, FOR ONE, YOU'RE DROOLING INTO THE FOOD.

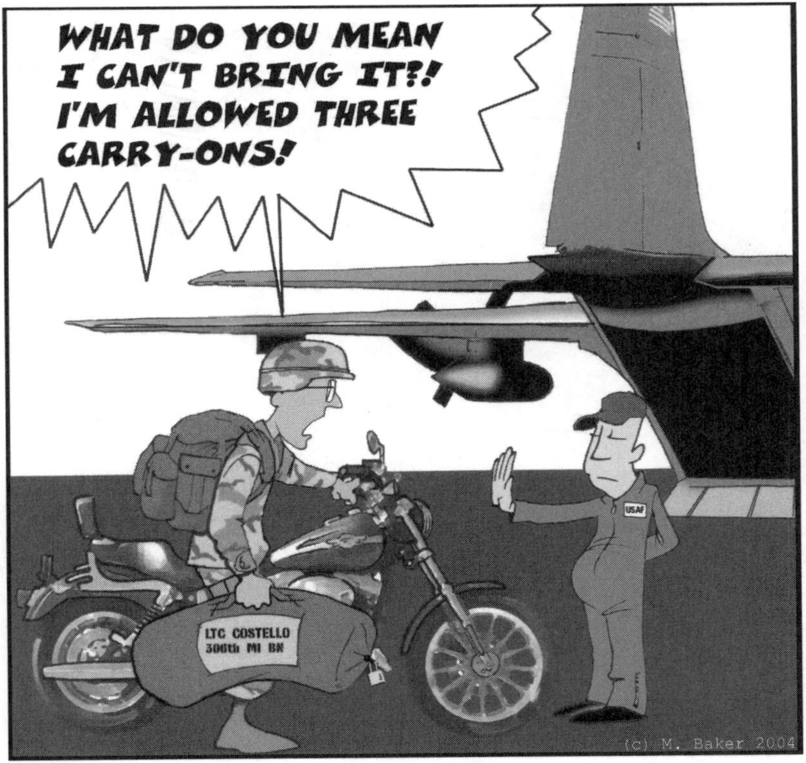
WHAT DO YOU MEAN I CAN'T BRING IT?! I'M ALLOWED THREE CARRY-ONS!
USAF
LTC COSTELLO
306th MI BN
(c) M. Baker 2004

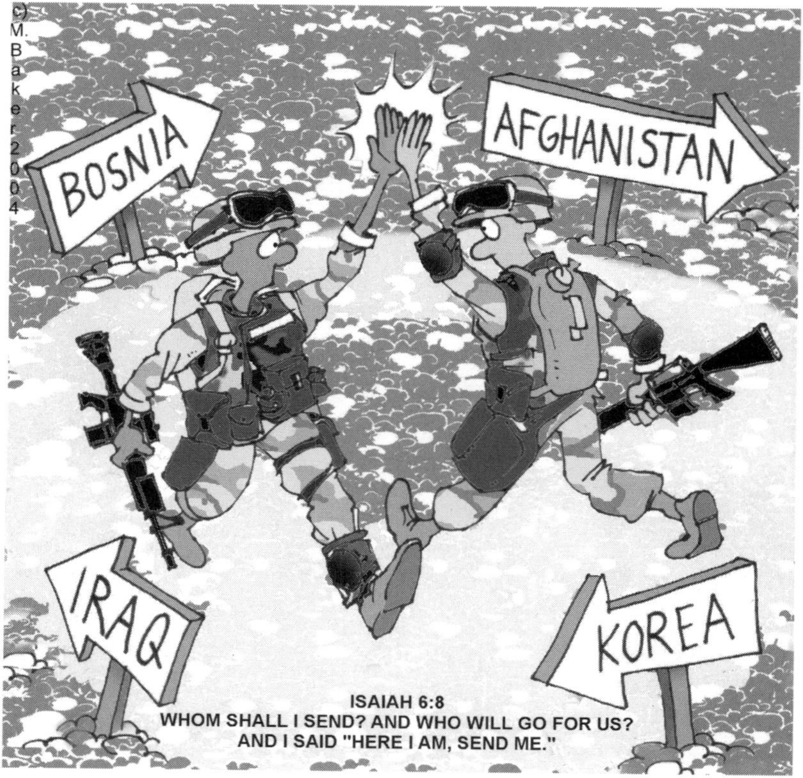
c) M. Baker 2004
BOSNIA
AFGHANISTAN
IRAQ
KOREA
ISAIAH 6:8
WHOM SHALL I SEND? AND WHO WILL GO FOR US?
AND I SAID "HERE I AM, SEND ME."

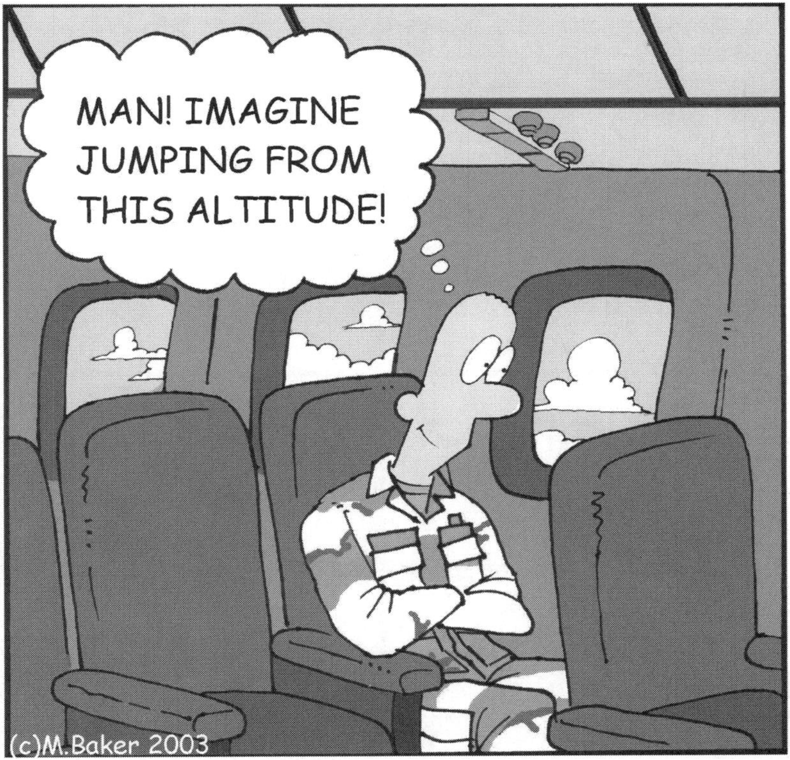
MAN! IMAGINE JUMPING FROM THIS ALTITUDE!
(c)M.Baker 2003

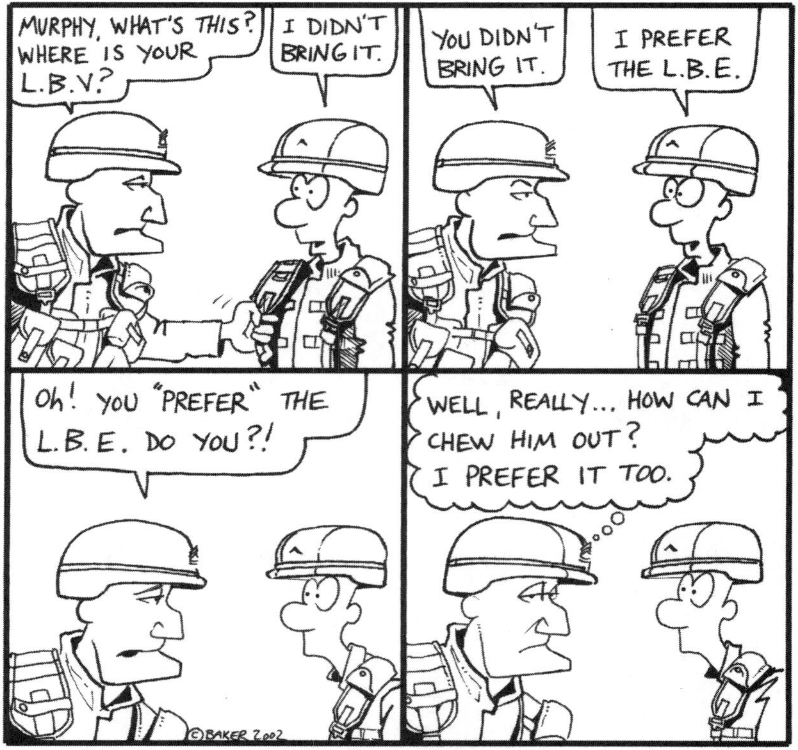

MURPHY, WHAT'S THIS? WHERE IS YOUR L.B.V.?
I DIDN'T BRING IT.
YOU DIDN'T BRING IT.
I PREFER THE L.B.E.
Oh! YOU "PREFER" THE L.B.E. DO YOU?!
WELL, REALLY... HOW CAN I CHEW HIM OUT? I PREFER IT TOO.
©BAKER 2002

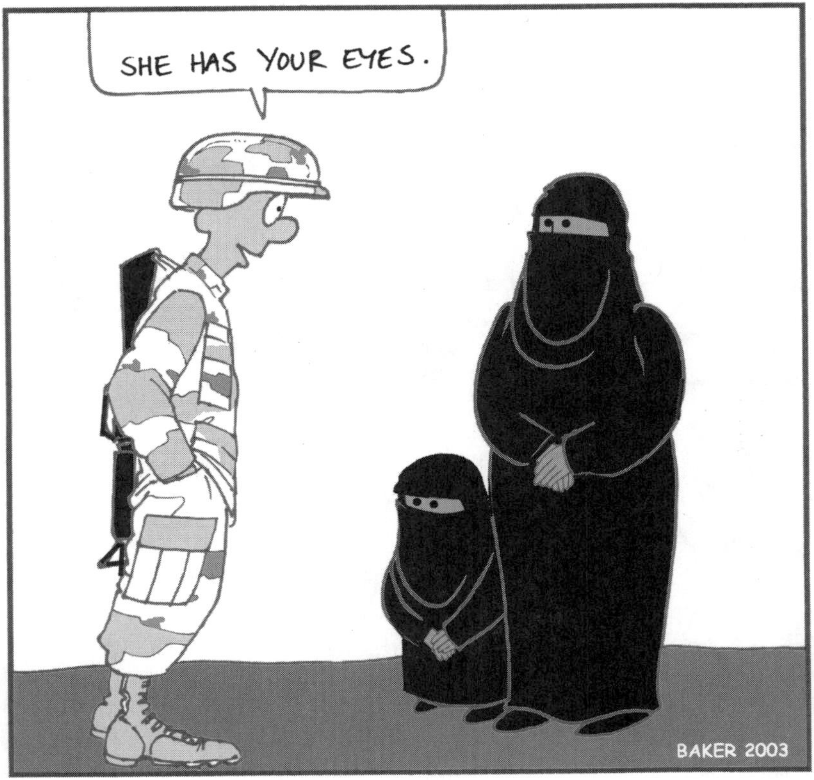
SHE HAS YOUR EYES.
BAKER 2003

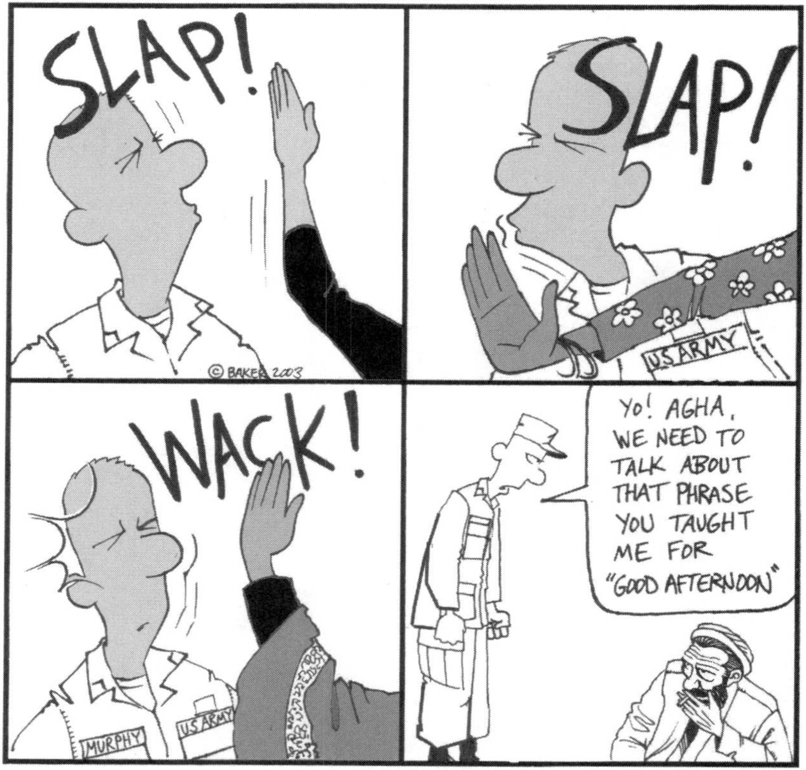
SLAP!
© BAKER 2003
SLAP!
U.S. ARMY
WACK!
MURPHY
U.S. ARMY
YO! AGHA, WE NEED TO TALK ABOUT THAT PHRASE YOU TAUGHT ME FOR "GOOD AFTERNOON"

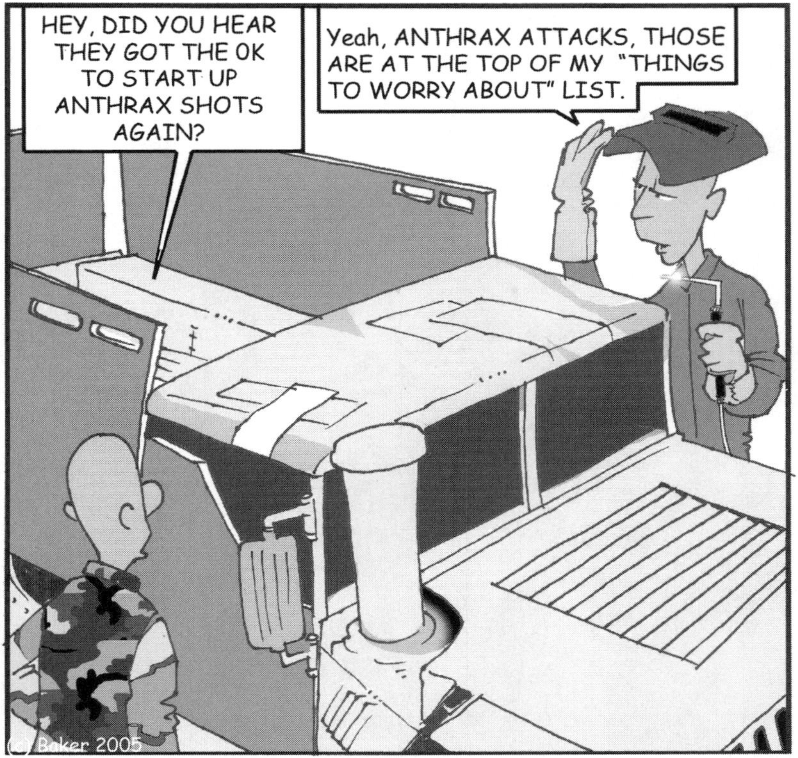
HEY, DID YOU HEAR THEY GOT THE OK TO START UP ANTHRAX SHOTS AGAIN?
Yeah, ANTHRAX ATTACKS, THOSE ARE AT THE TOP OF MY "THINGS TO WORRY ABOUT" LIST.
(c) Baker 2005

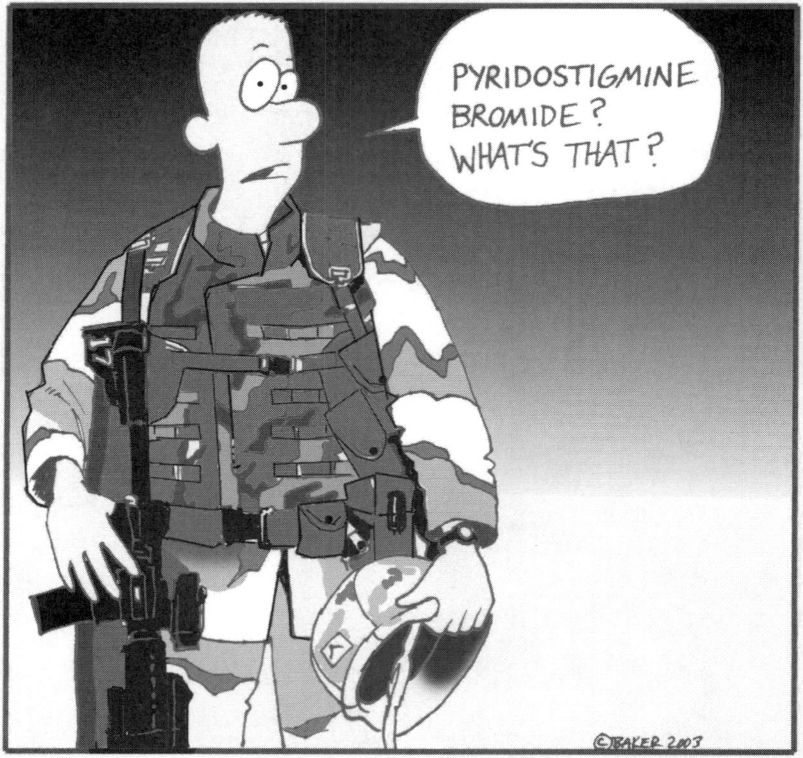
PYRIDOSTIGMINE BROMIDE? WHAT'S THAT?
©BAKER 2003

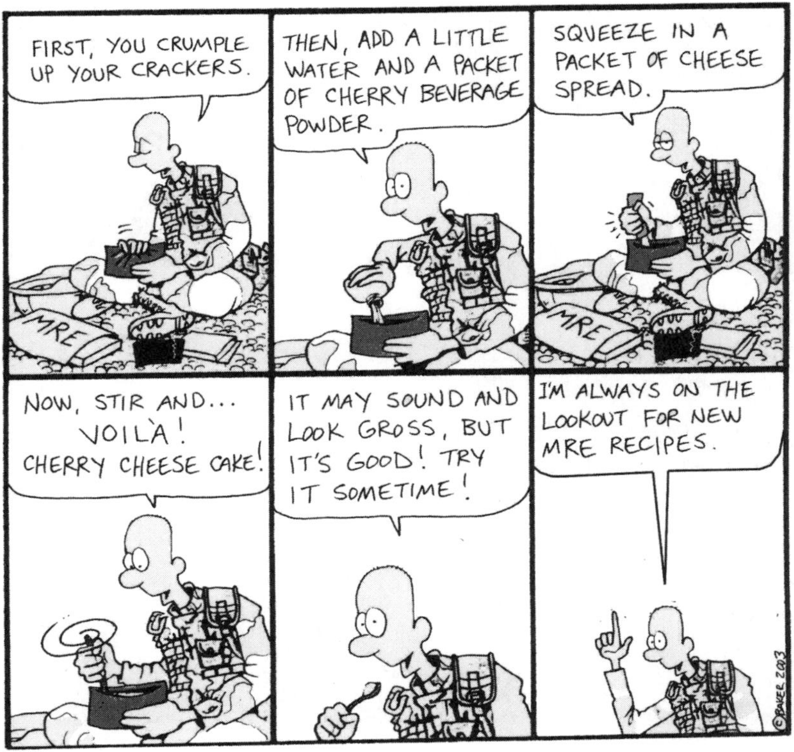
FIRST, YOU CRUMPLE UP YOUR CRACKERS.
THEN, ADD A LITTLE WATER AND A PACKET OF CHERRY BEVERAGE POWDER.
SQUEEZE IN A PACKET OF CHEESE SPREAD.
MRE
NOW, STIR AND... VOILÀ! CHERRY CHEESE CAKE!
IT MAY SOUND AND LOOK GROSS, BUT IT'S GOOD! TRY IT SOMETIME!
I'M ALWAYS ON THE LOOKOUT FOR NEW MRE RECIPES.
©BAKER 2003

This really works and it's good. (Good being a relative expression.)

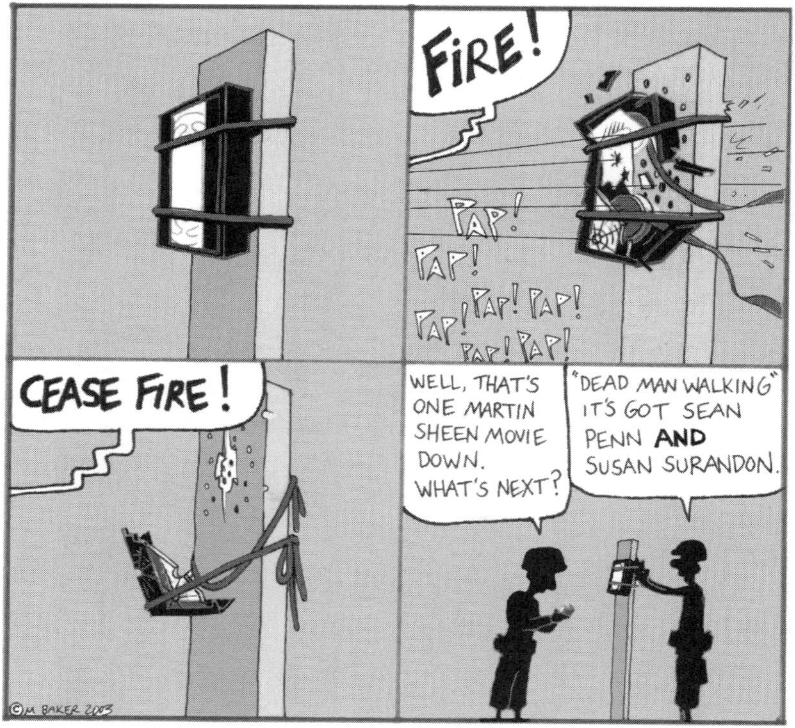
FIRE!
PAP! PAP! PAP! PAP! PAP! PAP! PAP!
CEASE FIRE!
WELL, THAT'S ONE MARTIN SHEEN MOVIE DOWN. WHAT'S NEXT?
"DEAD MAN WALKING" IT'S GOT SEAN PENN AND SUSAN SURANDON.
©M BAKER 2003

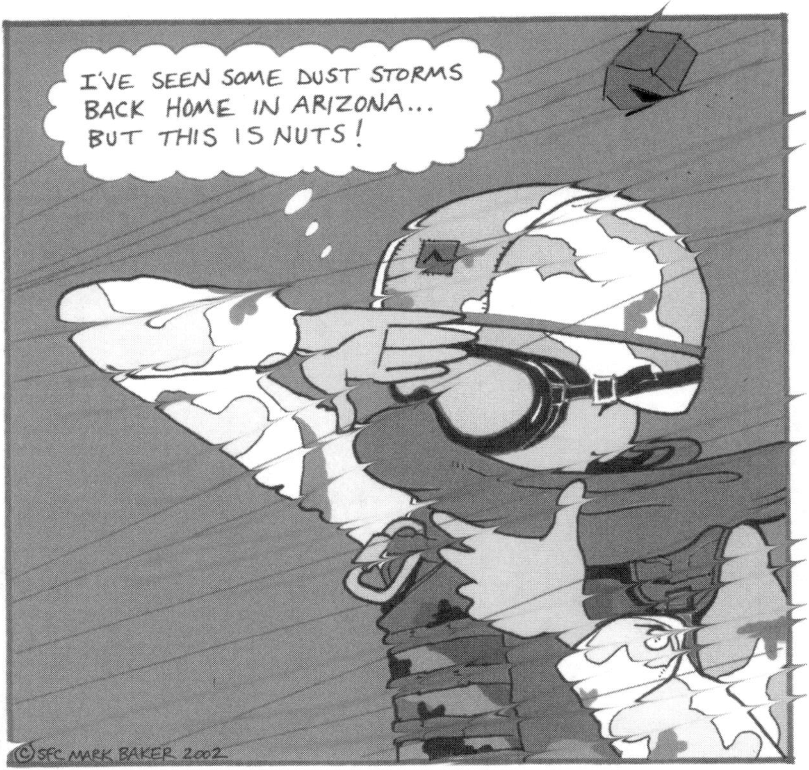
I'VE SEEN SOME DUST STORMS BACK HOME IN ARIZONA... BUT THIS IS NUTS!
©SFC MARK BAKER 2002

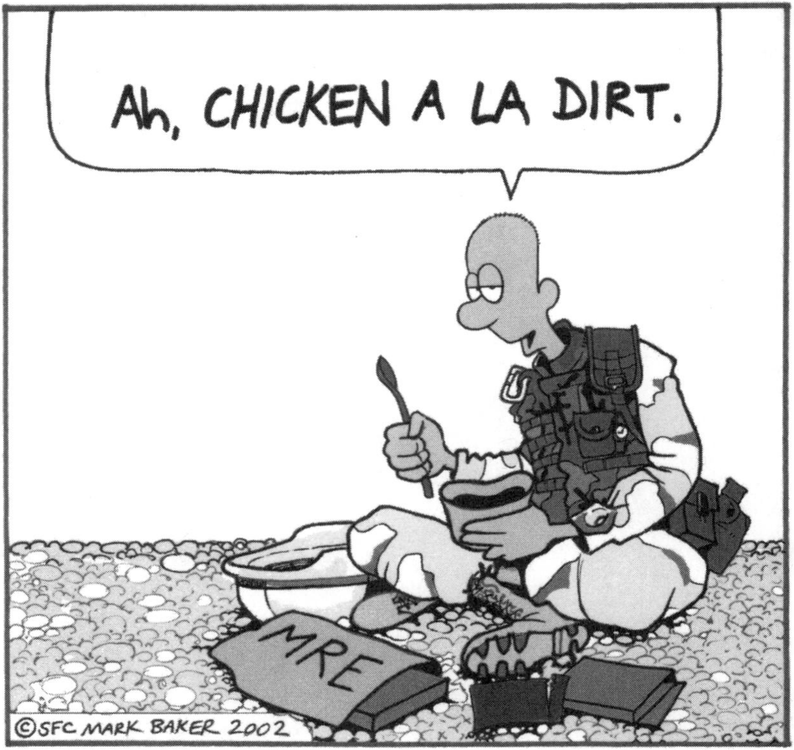
Ah, CHICKEN A LA DIRT.
MRE
©SFC MARK BAKER 2002

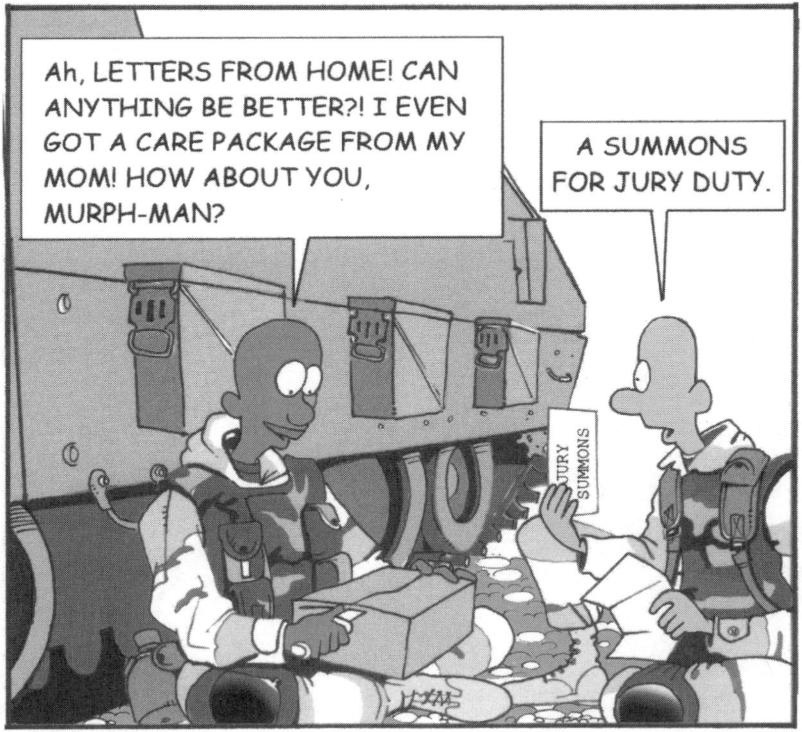
Ah, LETTERS FROM HOME! CAN ANYTHING BE BETTER?! I EVEN GOT A CARE PACKAGE FROM MY MOM! HOW ABOUT YOU, MURPH-MAN?
A SUMMONS FOR JURY DUTY.
JURY SUMMONS

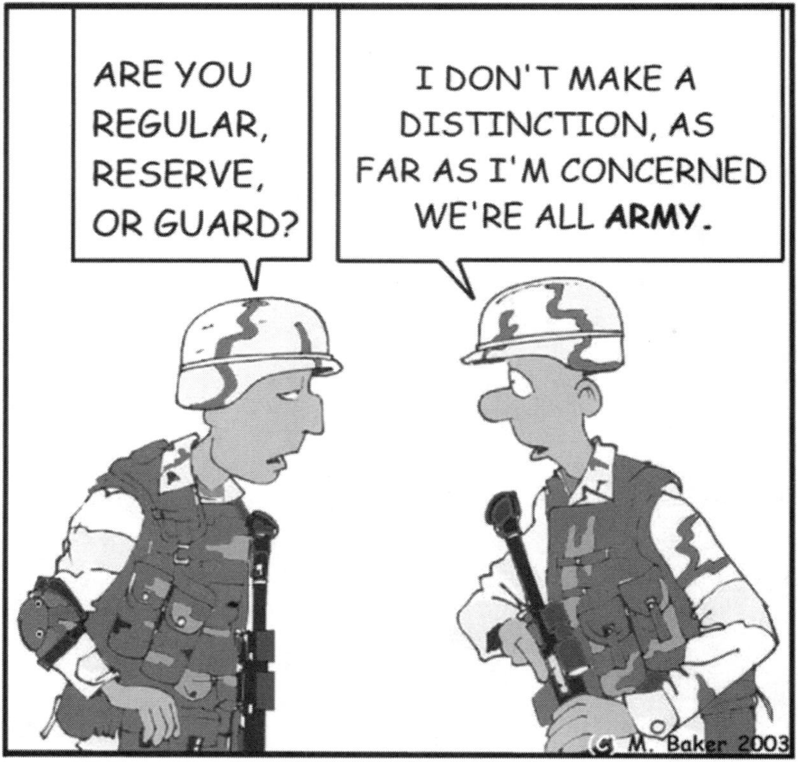
ARE YOU REGULAR, RESERVE, OR GUARD?
I DON'T MAKE A DISTINCTION, AS FAR AS I'M CONCERNED WE'RE ALL **ARMY**.
(C) M. Baker 2003

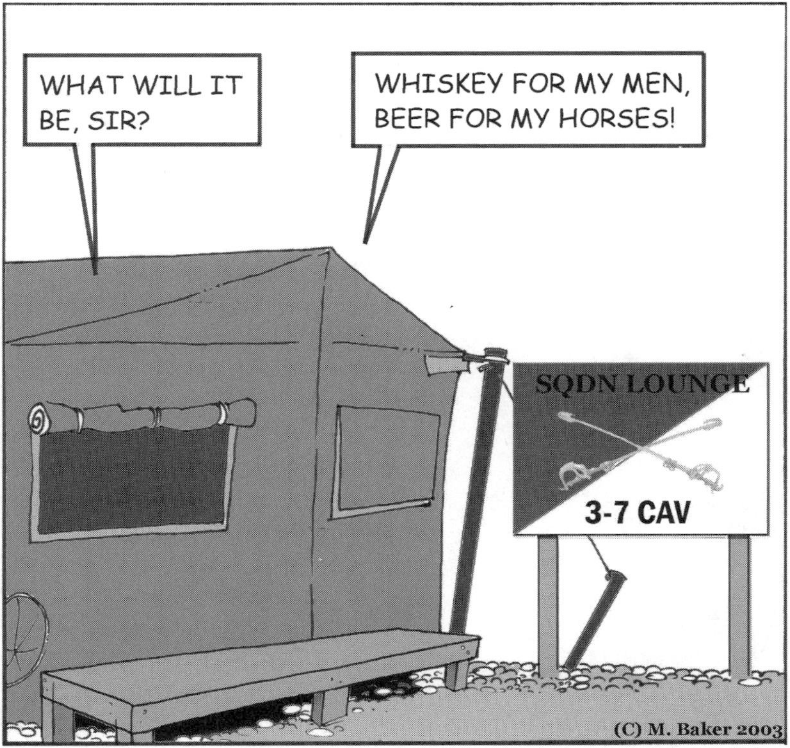
WHAT WILL IT BE, SIR?
WHISKEY FOR MY MEN, BEER FOR MY HORSES!
SQDN LOUNGE
3-7 CAV
(C) M. Baker 2003

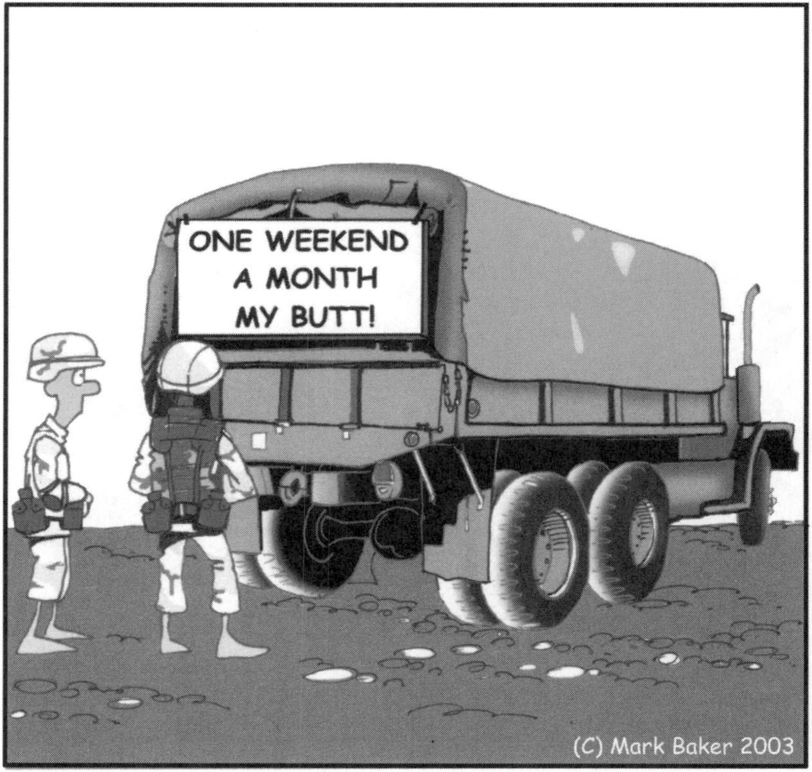
ONE WEEKEND
A MONTH
MY BUTT!
(C) Mark Baker 2003

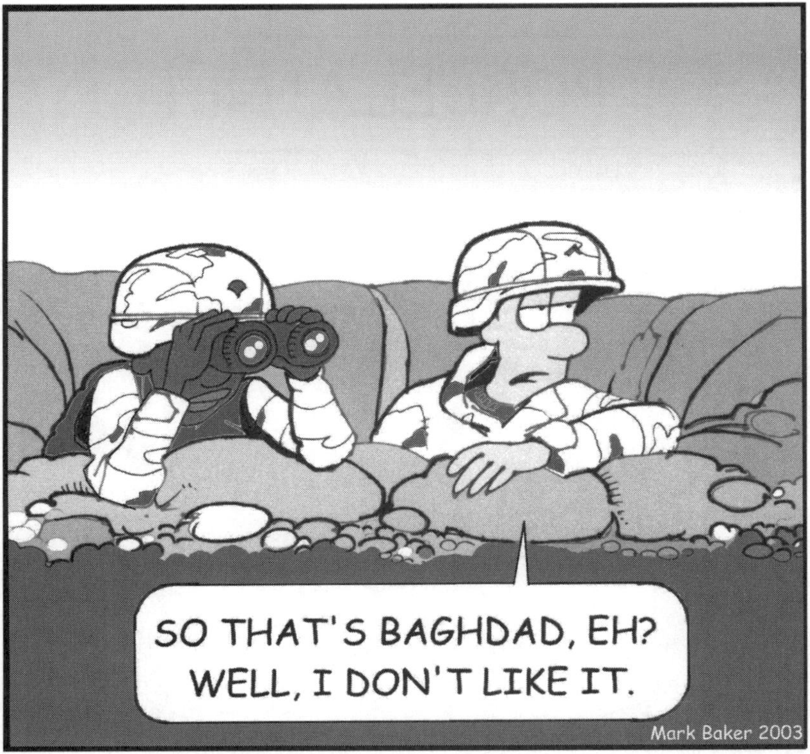
SO THAT'S BAGHDAD, EH? WELL, I DON'T LIKE IT.
Mark Baker 2003

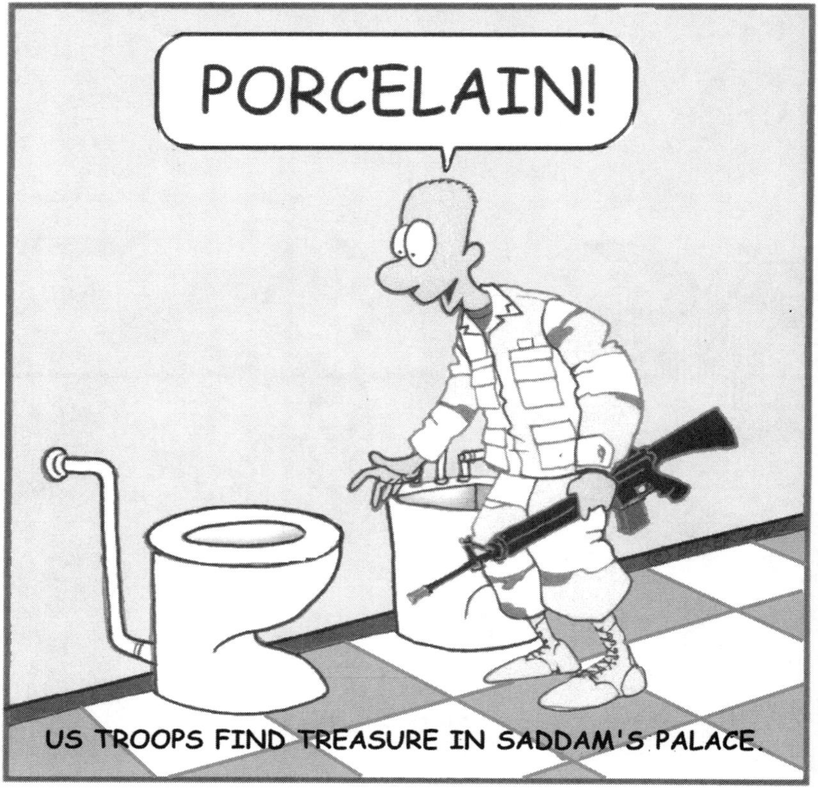
PORCELAIN!
US TROOPS FIND TREASURE IN SADDAM'S PALACE.

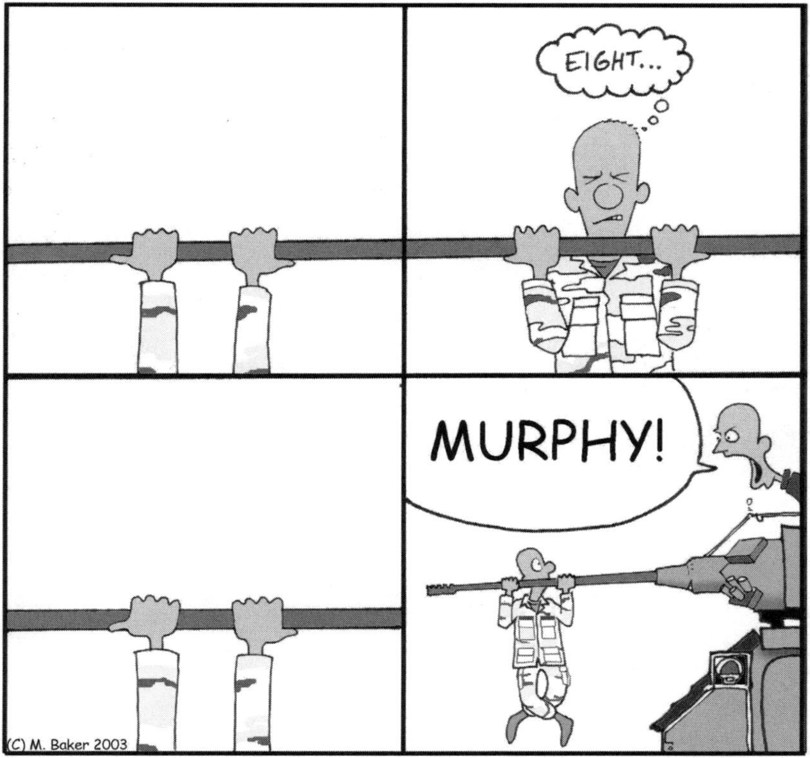
EIGHT...
MURPHY!
(C) M. Baker 2003

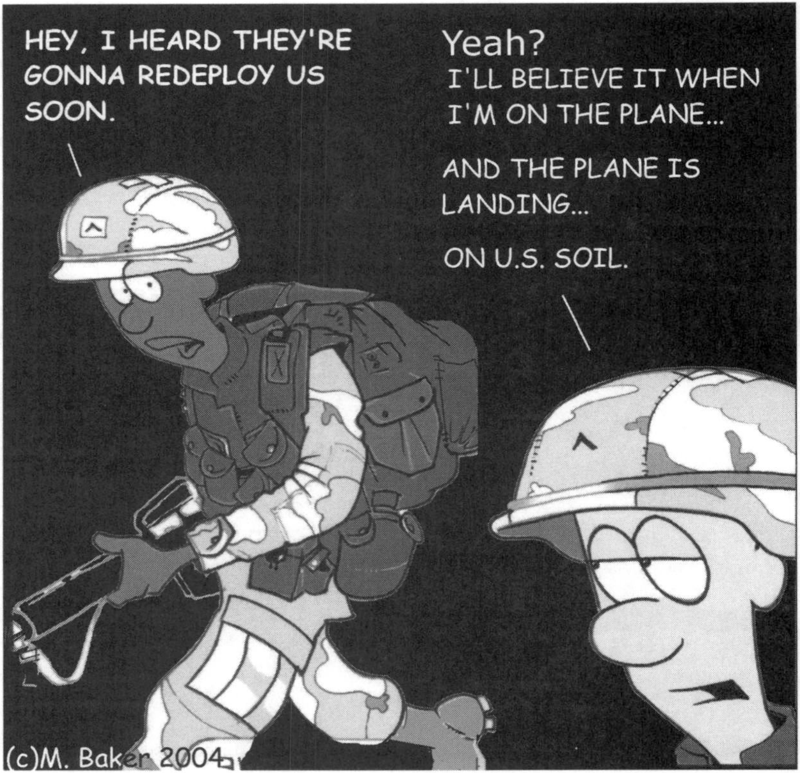
HEY, I HEARD THEY'RE GONNA REDEPLOY US SOON.
Yeah?
I'LL BELIEVE IT WHEN I'M ON THE PLANE...
AND THE PLANE IS LANDING...
ON U.S. SOIL.
(c)M. Baker 2004

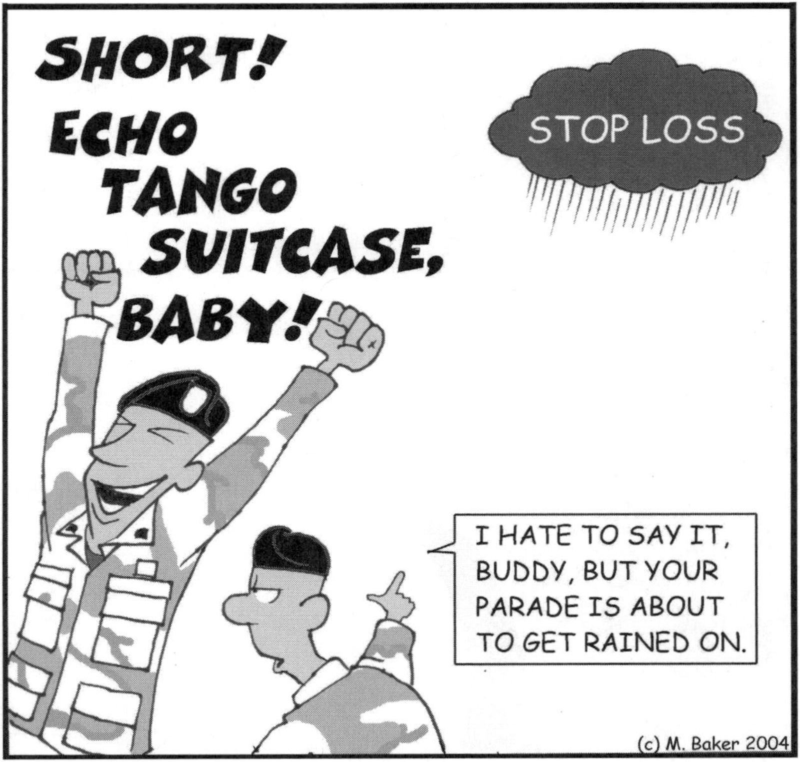
SHORT! ECHO TANGO SUITCASE, BABY!
STOP LOSS
I HATE TO SAY IT, BUDDY, BUT YOUR PARADE IS ABOUT TO GET RAINED ON.
(c) M. Baker 2004

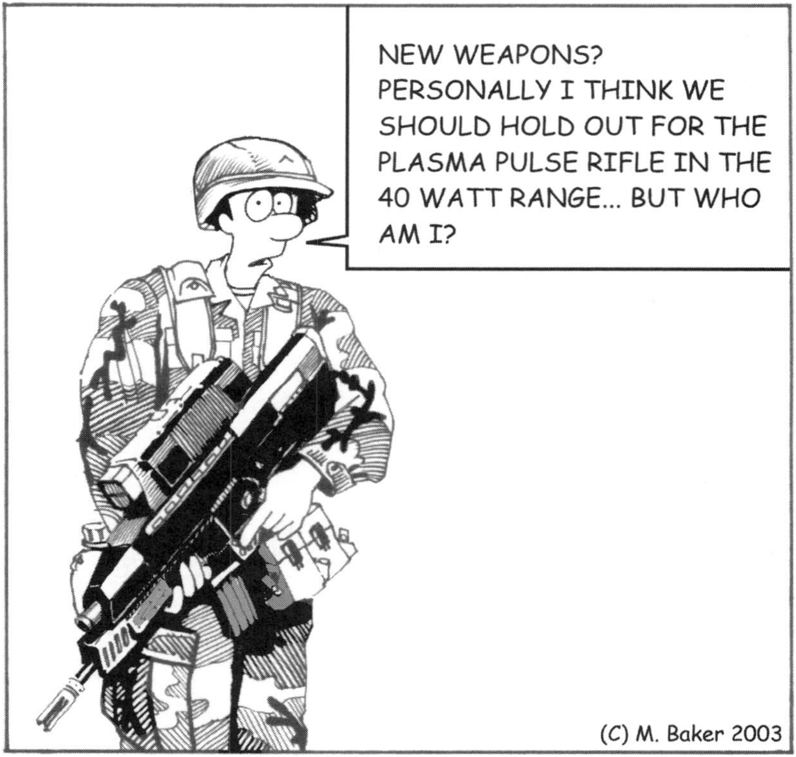
NEW WEAPONS? PERSONALLY I THINK WE SHOULD HOLD OUT FOR THE PLASMA PULSE RIFLE IN THE 40 WATT RANGE... BUT WHO AM I?
(C) M. Baker 2003

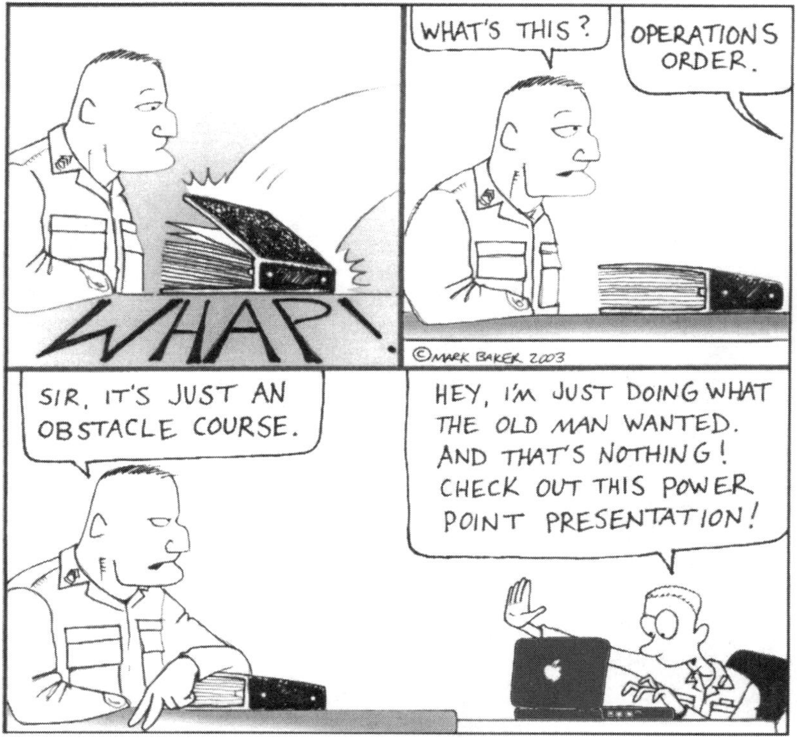
WHAP!
WHAT'S THIS?
OPERATIONS ORDER.
©MARK BAKER 2003
SIR, IT'S JUST AN OBSTACLE COURSE.
HEY, I'M JUST DOING WHAT THE OLD MAN WANTED. AND THAT'S NOTHING! CHECK OUT THIS POWER POINT PRESENTATION!

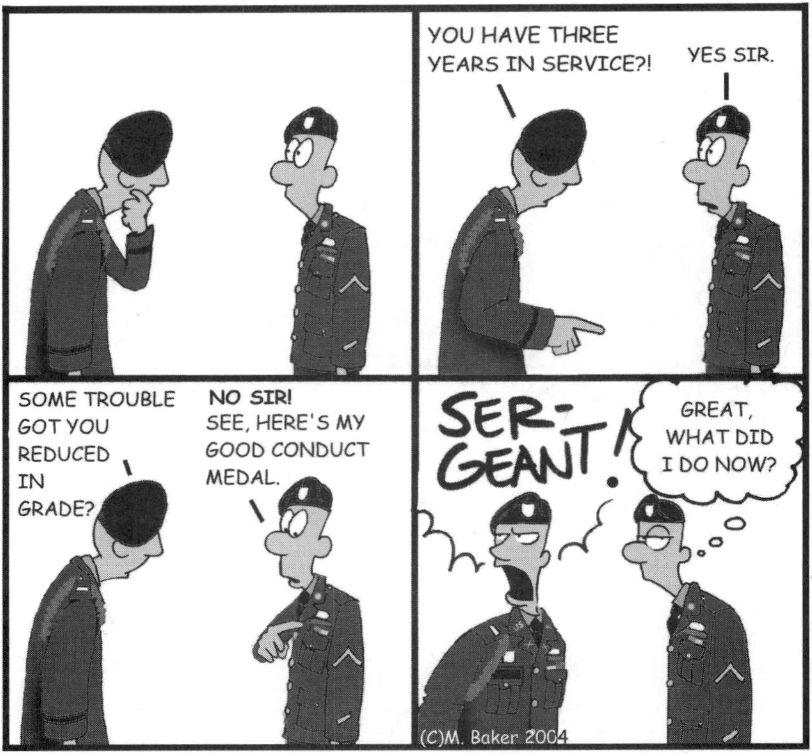
YOU HAVE THREE YEARS IN SERVICE?!
YES SIR.
SOME TROUBLE GOT YOU REDUCED IN GRADE?
NO SIR! SEE, HERE'S MY GOOD CONDUCT MEDAL.
SER-GEANT!
GREAT, WHAT DID I DO NOW?
(C)M. Baker 2004

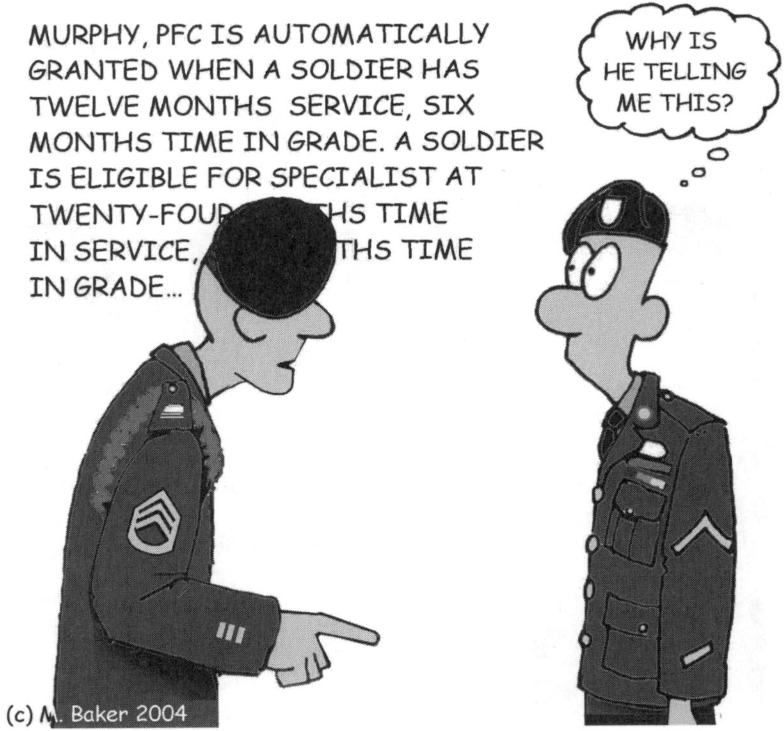
MURPHY, PFC IS AUTOMATICALLY GRANTED WHEN A SOLDIER HAS TWELVE MONTHS SERVICE, SIX MONTHS TIME IN GRADE. A SOLDIER IS ELIGIBLE FOR SPECIALIST AT TWENTY-FOU HS TIME IN SERVICE, THS TIME IN GRADE...
WHY IS HE TELLING ME THIS?
(c) M. Baker 2004

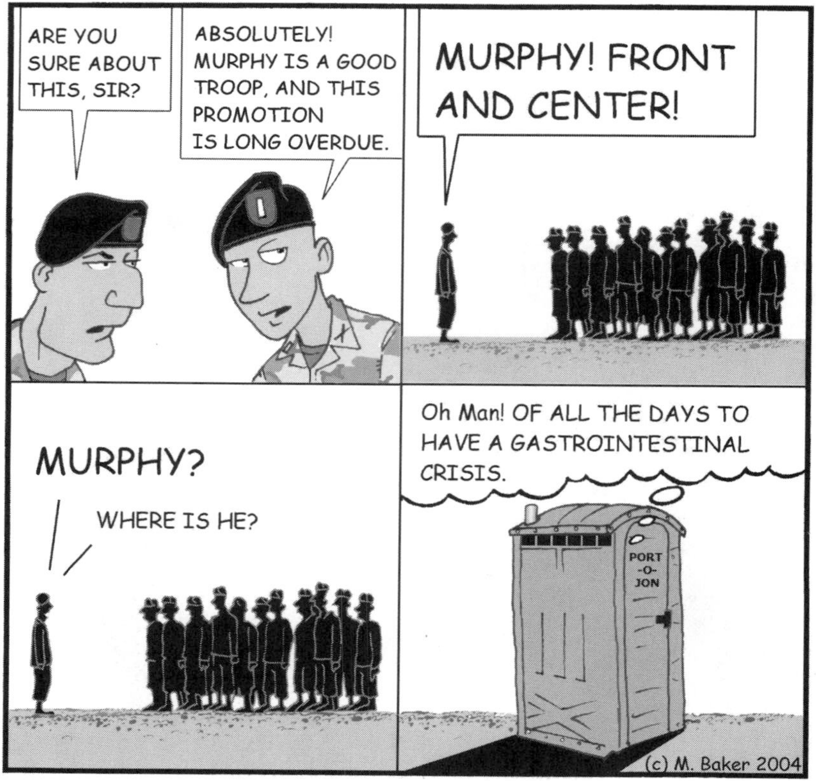
ARE YOU SURE ABOUT THIS, SIR?
ABSOLUTELY! MURPHY IS A GOOD TROOP, AND THIS PROMOTION IS LONG OVERDUE.
MURPHY! FRONT AND CENTER!
MURPHY?
WHERE IS HE?
Oh Man! OF ALL THE DAYS TO HAVE A GASTROINTESTINAL CRISIS.
PORT -O- JON
(c) M. Baker 2004

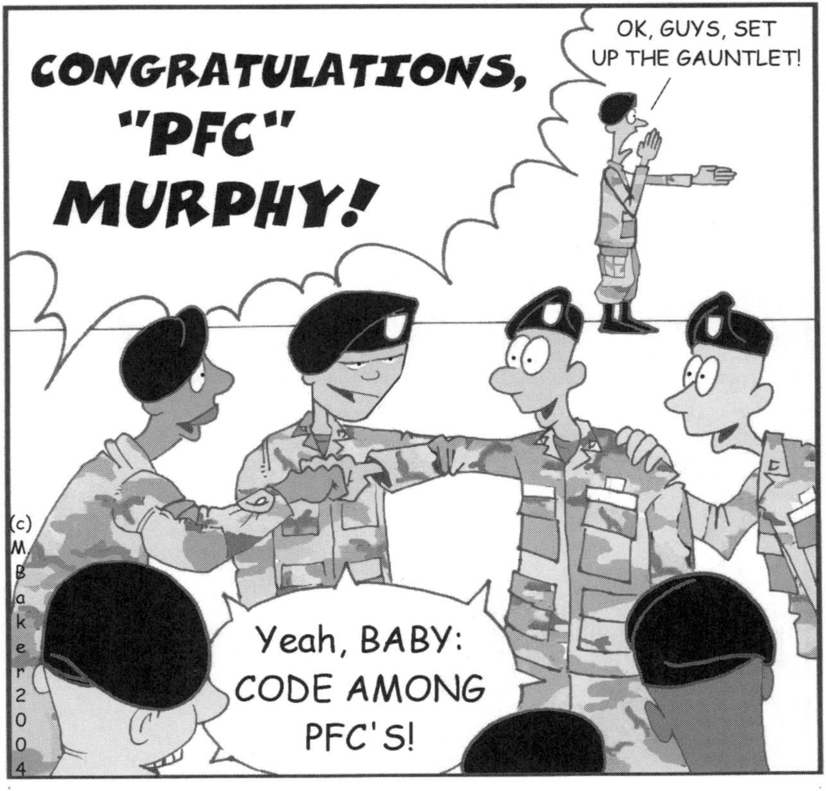
CONGRATULATIONS, "PFC" MURPHY!
OK, GUYS, SET UP THE GAUNTLET!
Yeah, BABY: CODE AMONG PFC'S!
(c) M. Baker 2004

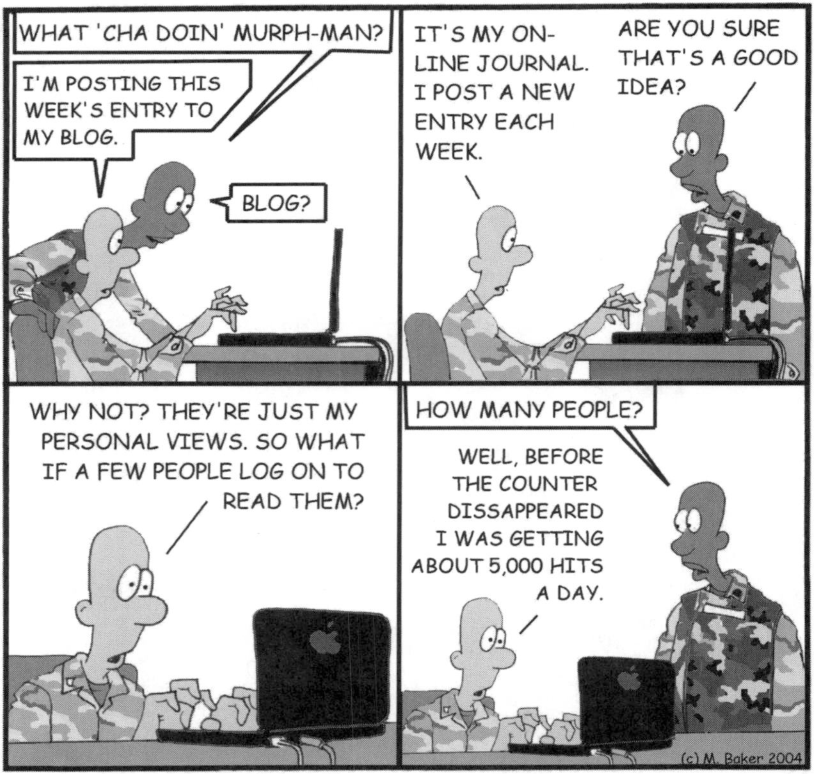
WHAT 'CHA DOIN' MURPH-MAN?
I'M POSTING THIS WEEK'S ENTRY TO MY BLOG.
BLOG?
IT'S MY ON-LINE JOURNAL. I POST A NEW ENTRY EACH WEEK.
ARE YOU SURE THAT'S A GOOD IDEA?
WHY NOT? THEY'RE JUST MY PERSONAL VIEWS. SO WHAT IF A FEW PEOPLE LOG ON TO READ THEM?
HOW MANY PEOPLE?
WELL, BEFORE THE COUNTER DISSAPPEARED I WAS GETTING ABOUT 5,000 HITS A DAY.
(c) M. Baker 2004

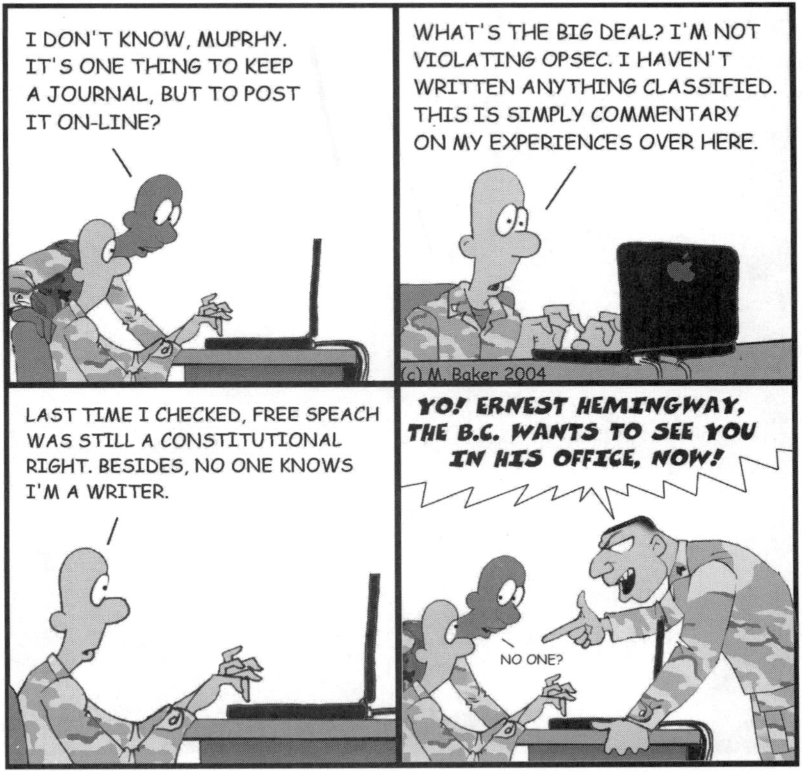
I DON'T KNOW, MUPRHY. IT'S ONE THING TO KEEP A JOURNAL, BUT TO POST IT ON-LINE?
WHAT'S THE BIG DEAL? I'M NOT VIOLATING OPSEC. I HAVEN'T WRITTEN ANYTHING CLASSIFIED. THIS IS SIMPLY COMMENTARY ON MY EXPERIENCES OVER HERE.
(c) M. Baker 2004
LAST TIME I CHECKED, FREE SPEACH WAS STILL A CONSTITUTIONAL RIGHT. BESIDES, NO ONE KNOWS I'M A WRITER.
YO! ERNEST HEMINGWAY, THE B.C. WANTS TO SEE YOU IN HIS OFFICE, NOW!
NO ONE?

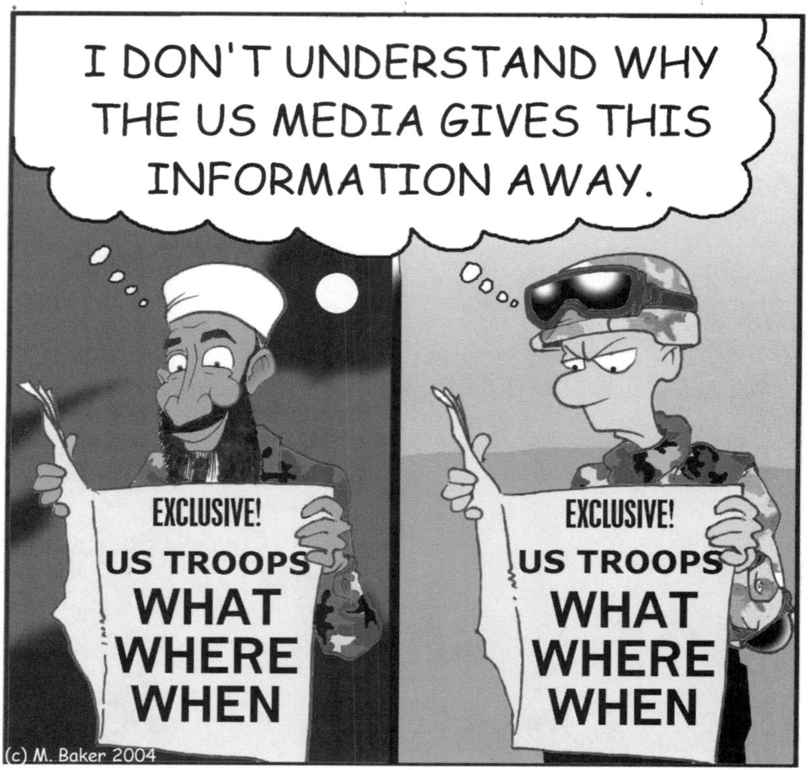
I DON'T UNDERSTAND WHY THE US MEDIA GIVES THIS INFORMATION AWAY.
EXCLUSIVE!
US TROOPS
WHAT
WHERE
WHEN
EXCLUSIVE!
US TROOPS
WHAT
WHERE
WHEN
(c) M. Baker 2004

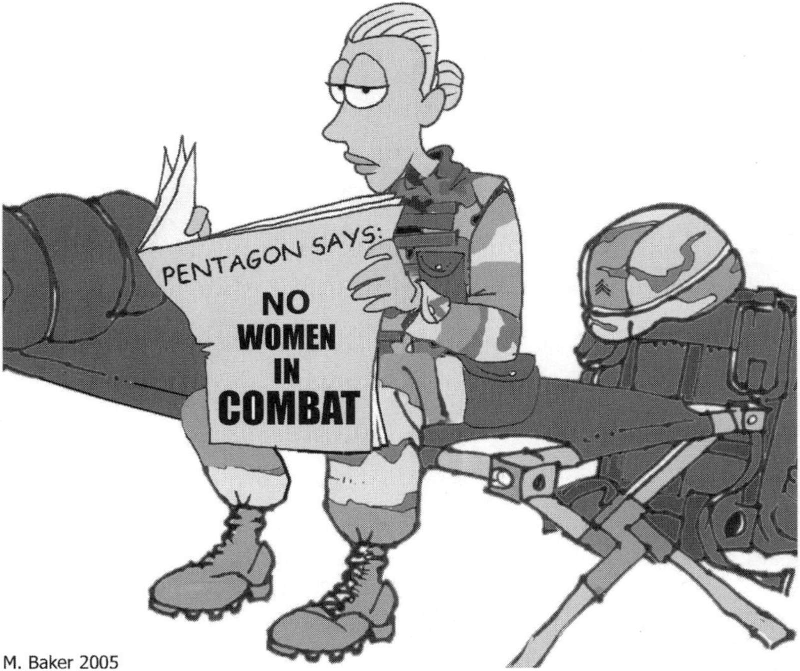
PENTAGON SAYS:
NO
WOMEN
IN
COMBAT

M. Baker 2005

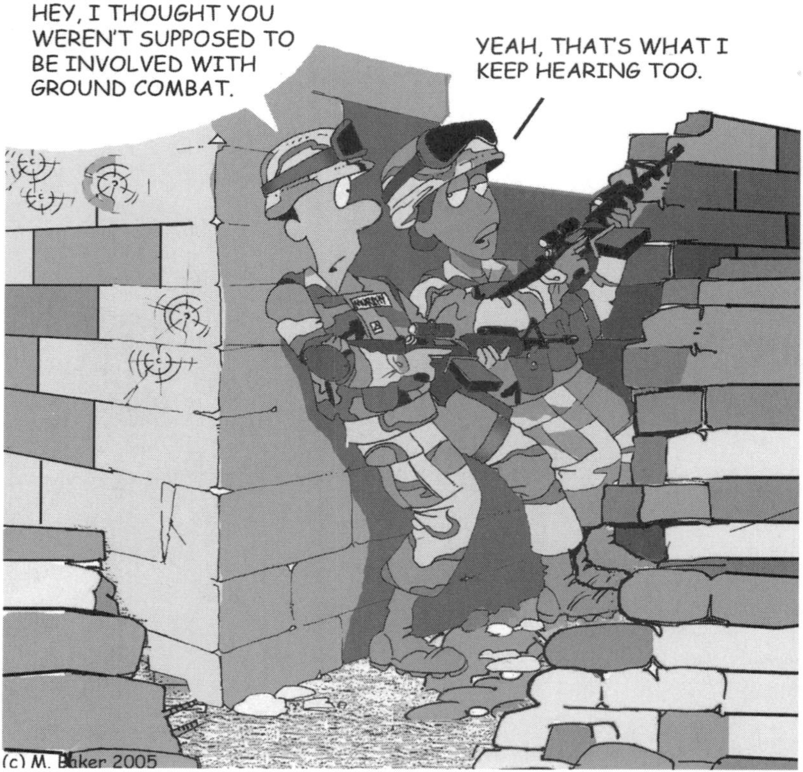
HEY, I THOUGHT YOU WEREN'T SUPPOSED TO BE INVOLVED WITH GROUND COMBAT.
YEAH, THAT'S WHAT I KEEP HEARING TOO.
(c) M. Baker 2005

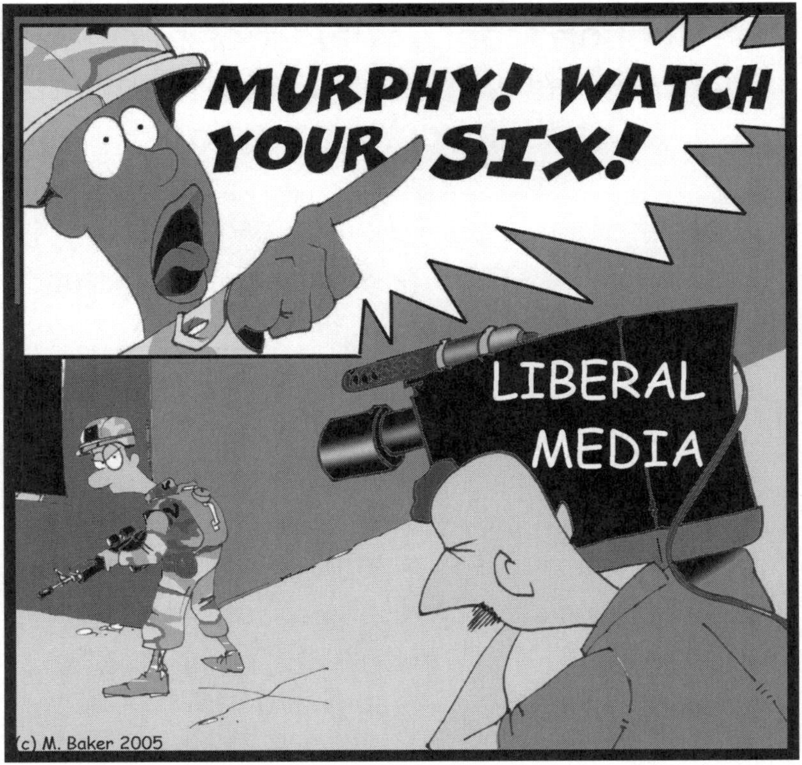
MURPHY! WATCH YOUR SIX!
LIBERAL MEDIA
(c) M. Baker 2005

Support Concurrent Receipt of Military Retirement Pay and Veterans Disability compensation

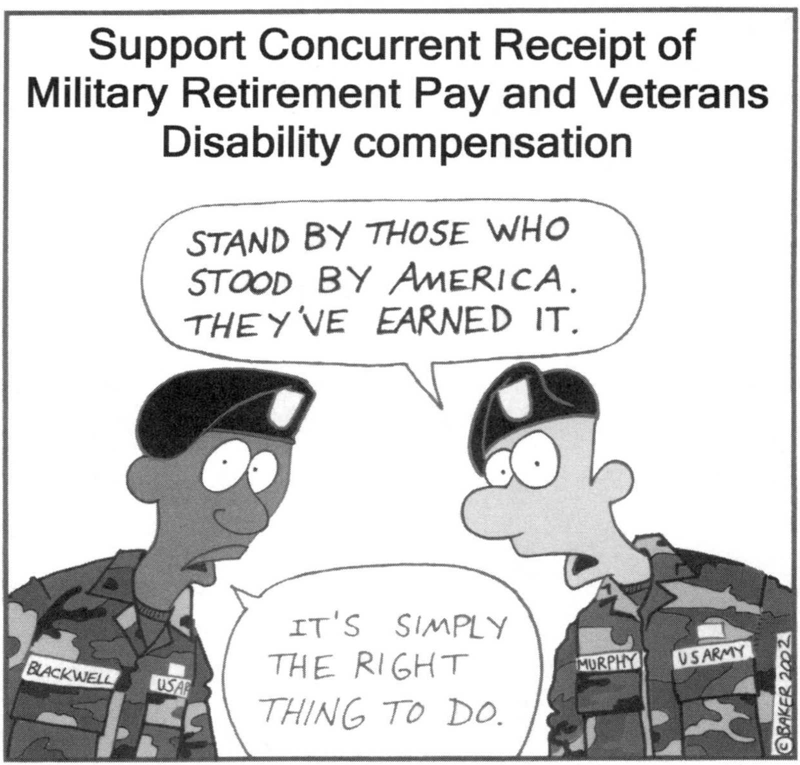
STAND BY THOSE WHO STOOD BY AMERICA. THEY'VE EARNED IT.
IT'S SIMPLY THE RIGHT THING TO DO.
BLACKWELL
USAF
MURPHY
U.S. ARMY
©BAKER 2002

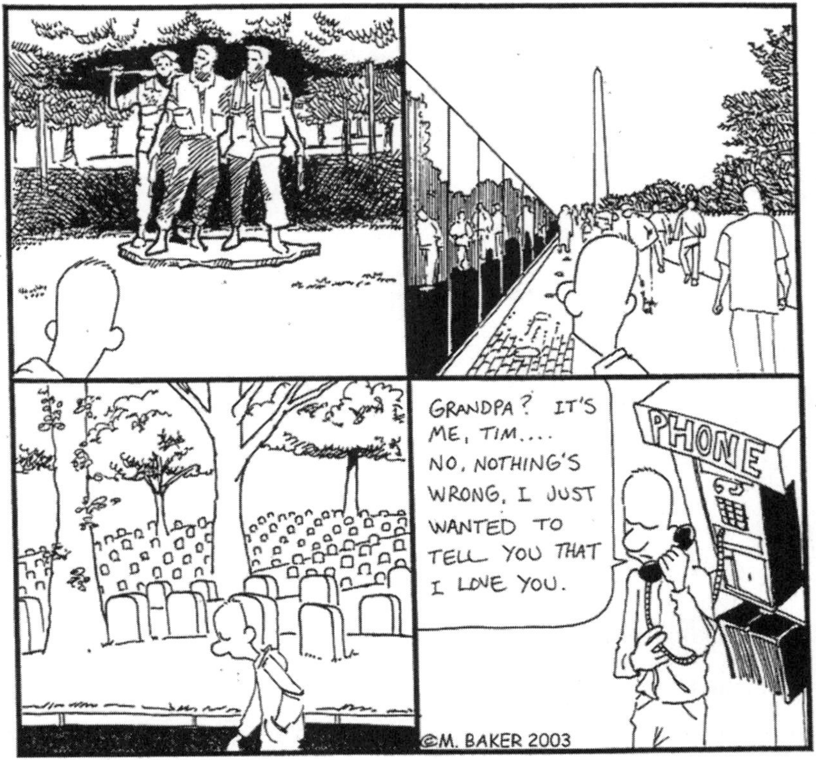
GRANDPA? IT'S ME, TIM.... NO, NOTHING'S WRONG. I JUST WANTED TO TELL YOU THAT I LOVE YOU.
PHONE
©M. BAKER 2003

Universal Press Syndicate

November 16, 2004

Mr. Mark V. Baker
106 A Fuller Street
Ft. Huachuca, AZ 85613

Dear Mr. Baker:

We have had an opportunity to consider the cartoon's *Pvt. Murphy's Law for* syndication.

While we find the consistency of your dialogue and artwork to be good, we'll have to pass. Our editorial board does not think we could do justice to your efforts.

I encourage you to pursue the idea with another syndicate, and appreciate you thinking of Universal Press.

Best regards.

Sincerely,

John Glynn
Acquisitions Editor

JG:lj